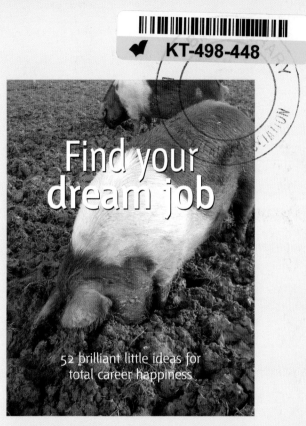

Find your dream job

52 brilliant little ideas for
total career happiness

Ken Langdon & John Middleton

brilliantideas

CAREFUL NOW

Follow the tips in this book and
you should find that you can
increase your earning power,
shine at work and most
importantly, enjoy your job.
But don't expect instant results.
The tips in this book are tried
and tested – they really do
work – but you'll have to
persevere, so no foot stamping
and angry emails if you don't
find everything going your way
instantly. Only you can find
yourself the job you dream of.
We wish you every success –
good luck!

Infinite Ideas would like to
thank Ken Langdon, Penny
Ferguson, Andrew Holmes, Jon
Smith, Tim Wright, Rob Bevan,
Tim Phillips, Steve Shipside and
John Middleton for their
contributions to this book.

First published in 2006 by
The Infinite Ideas Company Limited
36 St Giles
Oxford, OX1 3LD
United Kingdom
www.infideas.com

A CIP catalogue record for this book is available from the
British Library

ISBN 10: 1-904902-35-9
ISBN 13: 978-1-904902-35-5

Brand and product names are trademarks or registered
trademarks of their respective owners.

Designed and typeset by Baseline Arts Ltd, Oxford
Printed in Singapore

Brilliant ideas

Introduction 11

1. **Vocation, vocation** 13
Smart people recognise that learning
does not stop once formal education
finishes.

2. **Taking the test** 15
Would you mind taking a simple test to
see how you might fit in with your
colleagues?

3. **On your bike?** 17
Only one thing gets you down, and
hence stressed, more than work. Not
working.

4. **Putting you first** 19
Take a positive, practical but sceptical
attitude to your organisation. Don't
expect to spend your whole career in
one organisation and don't trip over
internal politics.

5. **Apply yourself** 21
The low-down on application forms

6. **Doing nothing at work – bosses** 24
Middle management is the natural
environment of choice for the serious
slacker...

7. **How do I look?** 26
Like it or not, your appearance and
your health are of more and more
interest to your employer.

8. **Back the right horse** 28
You need to get noticed. Identify who
is important to your progress, and get
to them. Sometimes that will mean
bypassing a human blockage.

9. **Show me the money** 30
Test your market value.

10. **Nothing fails like success** 32
Every great idea contains seeds of its
own failure.

11. **You are totally responsible for you** 34
It's a great mistake to think that anyone is as interested in your career as you are.

12. **Magnum opus** 36
Creating a business plan is like bearing your soul to the world.

13. **What's my line?** 38
Your career depends on your organisation meeting its objectives, and on you being seen as making a big contribution to those aims.

14. **Doing nothing at work – employees** 40
For run-of-the-mill workers, the key to loafing is to create an illusion of purpose and industry that deflects the scrutiny of superiors.

15. **Please find attached** 42
A top-notch covering letter can be viewed as either essential or totally unnecessary and we've no way of knowing which is the case.

16. **Ready, aim, fire** 45
Keeping someone in your team who plainly is not going to make it can be very bad for your career.

17. **Brass tacks...** 47
At some point you're going to have a somewhat technical discussion about the nitty-gritty of the job you're applying for. Make sure you get the detail right for your audience.

18. **Did someone say something?** ..49
Better your communication skills and you'll enhance your performance at work.

19. **Be organised** 51
How can you be sure that you're going to end the day having really *done* something?

20. **Leave on time** 53
Reduce interruptions. Reclaim your evenings. Take control.

21. **Changing horses mid-career** ...55
If you make a move to a new company your fellow managers there have an advantage over you...

22. **Persuasion** ...57
What's the most effective way of influencing people?

23. **Detox your CV** ...59
You don't get two chances to make a first impression, so remove any harmful content from your CV that might raise negative thoughts.

24. **Facing the inevitable question** 61
You know it's going to come up: 'So, why do you want this job?'

25. **Get your own way with a consultant** ...64
External consultants present both an opportunity and a threat to your career. Exploit the opportunity and avoid the threat by planning how and when to get involved with them.

26. **Cunning plans** ...66
Careerists need to treat a fluid list of complex activities as a project. Make sure you don't have one arm tied behind your back before you start.

27. **Working by the pool** ...68
For an ever-growing chunk of the population, working from home isn't a euphemism for skiving; it's a way of life.

28. **Networking** ...71
Exemplary networking is about quality of contacts, not quantity.

29. **Jump-start your salary** ...73
Do you deserve a higher salary? Well, of course you do. Let's look at tactics and techniques for making a persuasive case.

30. **Become a core competent** 76
If you want to be smart, build up your knowledge base. Tomorrow's world belongs to the 'core competents'.

31. **Dream a little dream** 78
Before putting pen to paper, consider what you want from the work you do.

32. **Glass ceiling?** 81
It's easier to get to the top if you are a man than if you're a woman. Here are some thoughts about how to deal with discrimination.

33. **Come back in the morning** 83
Know when to put things on the back-burner, and how to let them simmer there.

34. **Well read** 85
You need talent, artistry, political awareness and opportunism to enjoy the best your career can offer...

35. **Handling rejection** 87
A rejection letter needn't be the end of the story. A good follow-up strategy can keep you in the corporate mind's eye.

36. **Culture club** 90
You really are looking for compatibility. If the culture's not right, you'll eventually hate the job.

37. **Eight potentially life-changing seconds** 92
On average, it takes eight seconds to decide whether to continue reading a CV. Here's how to capture and keep the reader's attention in those first vital moments.

38. **Winging a meeting**.................95
There's a good reason why we don't prepare for meetings: we don't have time. Seriously. Don't bother.

39. **Life's a balance** 97
It's your choice whether to be a workaholic or not.

40. **How to love the job you've got** 99
Sometimes you can't have the one you want. So you have to love the one you've got.

41. **Who are they?** 101
Find out about your next potential employer and target your CV.

42. **Finding the perfect boss** 104
You don't want to end up with a boss you can't stand or, worse still, can't stand you.

43. **Manage the brand called You** 106
What makes you so special?

44. **Lead with style** 108
The ultimate test of leadership is the top job.

45. **Be an achiever** 110
A substantial record of personal achievements is more important than an impressive job description.

46. **Office politics** 112
Someone who says they're not interested in office politics is someone who's not going up the organisation as far as their talent deserves.

47. **Actions speak louder than decisions** 114
If you have taken a decision and informed your boss of what you and your team are going to do, for your career's sake make absolutely sure it happens.

48. **Downshifting**........................116
We all fantasise about chucking in the day job from time to time.

49. **The seven deadly CV sins**...... 118
Sometimes best practice is about the things we do; sometimes it's more about the things we don't do...

50. **Know what to say to whom**..120
A meteoric careerist can't have too much exposure to top people.

51. **Practical interview skills**.......122
Two items that often come up in second interviews or assessment centres are in-tray exercises and presentations.

52. **Jumping ship** 125
Here's how to get another job with a fat-cat salary when in your current job you've done nothing, nada, nix, and until now you've got away with it.

Introduction

You've always had a dream job, right? When
you were a kid it was probably something you
perceived as exciting and glamorous such as
fighter pilot, ballerina or spaceman. Perhaps
you achieved that – though you probably wouldn't be reading this
book if you had.

What's more likely is that your plans matured as you grew older and
working life became a reality. The more ambitious amongst us now
want to know how to make the CEO's office our own, while at the
other end of the scale there are those of us who just want to know
how to get through the working day as unscathed as possible and
still have time for all those other things that make up our lives –
family, friends, leisure time (little things like that).

Whichever one of these categories you fall into, and most of us are
somewhere between the two, there will be ideas in here to help
you. From crafting your first CV, through tackling the toughest of
interview questions to maintaining the job you have and progressing

in your career, it's all here. There are some tips for those of you who want to find ways of making a seemingly intolerable job better and even hints for anybody who wants it all – but wants to get there with the minimum of effort.

The beauty of this book is that all the information is here in ideas that take less time to read than your average bathroom- or cigarette-break. But don't let the shortness of the ideas fool you. Each one is brilliant and could help you improve your working life on its own. Taken together all 52 ideas could really help you find (and keep) your dream job.

1. Vocation, vocation

Smart people recognise that learning does not stop once formal education finishes.

Vocational exams are designed to cover a narrow subject to a much greater depth of understanding than broad academic exams. In some cases, they can be very narrow indeed.

Vocational courses are designed to make you more competent in a subject. As a result they are often practical and you will be expected to apply the skills directly after completing the course. It's been said that academic courses are there to broaden your mind whilst vocational courses are there to deepen your competence and expertise.

Another difference is that you tend to study for academic courses in your teens and early twenties, but most vocational study is undertaken once you are in work, and hence in your twenties, thirties, forties... and vocational courses tend to be shorter, often

Here's an idea for you...

Keep a logbook of examples of how you will be able to apply the skills you are learning to your job. This will help you in two ways. First, it will make what you are learning feel very real, and secondly it will help you apply the skills you have learnt more easily when you are back in the office.

13

Defining idea

'What we have to learn to do, we learn by doing.'
ARISTOTLE

lasting only a few weeks, and so your study is concentrated over a much shorter time frame. If it ends in an exam, you will have less time to revise, so this means that your study skills have to be in tip-top condition.

So what are the skills you need to succeed in vocational study? First and foremost is the ability to listen, interpret and apply what you have learnt to real-world situations; it's practicalities, not theories, that count in this kind of course. Secondly, you will need to be able to get to the point far more quickly in any exam because the subject matter is much narrower than what you might have been used to. The questions you will be set will be more direct and they will expect a direct answer. Thirdly, you will be expected to draw on your own experience to a much greater degree than in your early years of studying. And finally, the nature of the course will involve a lot more time thinking through particular problems and case studies, so there will be a need to interact a lot more, work in teams and apply what you have just learnt almost immediately. Vocational study is much less passive than academic courses.

2. Taking the test...

Would you mind taking a simple test to see how you might fit in with your colleagues?

Recruiters use tests because there's an intrinsic fallibility in making decisions based on interviews. The rapport that does or doesn't exist between interviewer and interviewee can lead to the wrong conclusion.

One type of test is the **personality test**. The good news about these tests is that there are no right or wrong answers and they're rarely done against the clock. The recruiter is generally looking for some further evidence of whether or not you will fit the role and the company and, of course, whether it will fit you.

The only thing to do here is to be honest. Answer the questions as accurately as you can and you'll probably enjoy it. Don't try to make out you're different from who you are. If you do, you'll be caught out in one of three ways: the test will pick it up, the test results won't fit with the data on you from the interview or you'll be offered the job on false pretences and will be found out when you're in the role.

Here's an idea for you...

Your answers will typically be looked at against a norm table of hundreds of people who have done the same test and a 'profile' will emerge which shows how you compare with the 'norm'. The company will seek to establish whether your profile matches what they need for a particular role now and in the future. Typically, it will explore areas like your sociability, ability to manage in a stressful situation, degree of inventiveness, and attitude to working in a team.

The other type of test is an **ability test**. Again, your responses will be compared with a norm group so the company can see if you work with facts, figures and data more effectively than X% of the population. It's important to get the accuracy/speed balance correct, since most of these tests are timed. Try not to sacrifice accuracy for speed. Most testers would rather see ten correct answers out of eleven rather than ten right out of twenty. However, don't take too long about it. If you only answer ten out of twenty you can't get more than 50%. Try to find out from the HR people whether they're going to ask you to do a test and if so which one.

Other ability tests look at your creativity or dexterity, among many other topics. Take a few deep breaths, keep calm and concentrate.

Do read the questions carefully; if you're going to be wrong, be wrong because you don't know, not because you misread the question. Finally, get feedback if you can, especially if you're sitting the tests before the interview. You have one arm tied behind your back if you don't.

3. On your bike?

Only one thing gets you down, and hence stressed, more than work. Not working.

Anyone basically who doesn't get paid (not who doesn't work) – is vulnerable to the stress of the 'no work' phenomenon. What's the answer?

If you're looking for a job, don't fritter away time worrying. You need a strategy. You need short-term and long-term goals. You need to break these goals down into tasks and you need to schedule these tasks in your diary.

Look into part-time or casual work that will at least give you some money until you get a job. Having lists of tasks completed will give you a sense of achievement and help you feel in control. Call every

Here's an idea for you...

Aim for excellence. You may be an adequate cook. Use your time 'off' to become a brilliant one. You may love reading. Become an exemplary reader. Read all those classic novels you've been meaning to devour but never got round to.

contact you know. The hardest thing in the world is to call ten contacts and sell yourself to them, but asking a friend to ring you to check that you've done it is a powerful motivator.

If you're at home with children, structure is vital. Set yourself personal goals – just like you did at work. These goals should not just be about the children.

Ask five people that know you well to answer these questions honestly:

- What is the first thing you think of when you think of me?
- What do you think is the most interesting thing about me?
- What do you think has been my greatest accomplishment?
- What do you value most about me?
- What do you perceive to be my greatest strengths?

OK. A bit embarrassing. But just say you've been asked to answer these questions on a job application and you're stuck for ideas. You'll be amazed at the different perceptions people have of you, and it helps you realise that qualities you take for granted aren't qualities that everyone shares. You're unique.

When you're short of money, isolated and bored, it's unlikely that you're getting the regular doses of endorphins that we need to stay happy campers. Understimulation leads to fatigue and depression. It's essential to manufacture highs and you have to do it daily. Make a 'joy list' of things that will give you a sense of achievement and happiness that don't cost a lot. Every day must have one pure pleasure.

Defining idea

'You take my life when you do take the means whereby I live.'

WILLIAM SHAKESPEARE, *The Merchant of Venice*

4. Putting you first

Don't expect to spend your whole career in one organisation and don't trip over internal politics.

Make sure you are working for an organisation that is doing something worthwhile and is likely to be successful. You are much more likely to build a career there. If right now you're working towards a goal that neither interests you nor inspires you, you've got to make a change. It's up to you. Your career is a key element in your way of life and your general happiness, so if you are in the wrong place get out of it.

Here's an idea for you...

It is best for your boss to think that other people believe your good ideas are his or hers. On the other hand, you want people to know that your ideas and your boss's good ideas are both yours.

Your organisation is probably chaotic, either all the time, or sometimes, or in places. This is both a problem and an opportunity for the career-minded. This chaos means that whatever it says about looking after you and your career, your company may very well not be able to live up to its promises. Organisations, for example, have to take technological change on board if they are to survive even if it costs careers. In short, the organisation has to look after itself in a businesslike way, so you need to look after yourself in a similarly objective and professional way.

The organisation is also not totally honest with its customers, or with its suppliers and regulators, or with its people, even if it means to be. Circumstances change. A promise made to a member of staff in good faith may suddenly become impractical. In this environment the safest view to take of your organisation is that you owe it your loyal support only for as long as your objectives and the organisation's can co-exist.

Companies no longer offer jobs for life and most successful careerists will change employers from time to time. Keep an open mind and remember that the 'company man' is extinct. The key phrase now is 'fluidity of labour'.

It's not possible for any organisation to exist without some form of internal politics. Don't make a decision on behalf of an organisation without paying attention to what the implications are for you. If company politics permeate every decision that affects your career, you should face another brutal fact: in company politics the competition is your colleagues. After all, this is more than a matter of survival. Take responsibility for your own career, and work on the basis that no one else will.

5. Apply yourself

The low-down on application forms.

From an organisation's perspective application forms can be a nifty way to reduce the time and money spent. Advertisements that ask for an application form to be completed typically have a lower response rate than those requesting CVs.

Fewer applicants can mean a lower-quality field, so if you can face the prospect of completing an application form without losing the will to live, you'll find that you'll typically be up against a smaller field of competition.

Here are some reasons why organisations like application forms:

- They ask all candidates for the same information and are regarded as good equal opportunities practice.
- They allow a readier comparison between candidates because every candidate is completing an identical form.

Now some tips on completing them:

- It makes sense to take a photocopy of the form so that you can draft out a rough version first. Multiple crossings out and handwriting that becomes increasingly smaller as you desperately try to squeeze your brilliant prose into a tiny space on the form don't go down a bundle with the personnel department.
- Use a black or dark blue pen – light turquoise ink may hint at your creative side, but it's a bugger to read and just as bad to photocopy.
- Ask yourself what the recruiting organisation is looking for in the right candidate. Then tailor the information you provide accordingly.

Here's an idea for you...

Although it might be tempting to simply send your CV with the form, with 'See my CV' written in as many sections as possible, you'll come over as both lazy and disinterested if you do this.

- Answer the questions as fully as possible, but don't waffle. Show that you can organise and express your thoughts clearly.
- There's normally a section of the application form that gives you an opportunity to make a personal statement. Use every last inch of it (and continue on a separate sheet if you need to). This might be your least favourite part of an application form, and it will almost certainly take the longest to complete, but it's a major opportunity to distinguish yourself from the competition.
- Take a copy for yourself before you post it.
- Knock up a short covering letter to go with the application form. Remember to quote the reference number and say where you saw the advert.
- Use an A4 envelope so that the application turns up uncrumpled at the other end.

Defining idea

'Perseverance is a great element of success. If you only knock long enough and loud enough at the gate, you are sure to wake somebody.'
HENRY WADSWORTH LONGFELLOW

6. Doing nothing at work – bosses

Middle management is the natural environment of choice for the serious slacker...

A survey by Investors in People recently found that 84% of workers in organisations with more than 1000 employees thought they had a lazy colleague. That compared with only 50% in companies with fewer than fifty staff. It probably comes down to the simple truth that small companies don't have middle management.

Here's an idea for you...

To really make the grade as a slacker boss, you will need a 'treasure' – an assistant who actually does some of the things you should do, keeps your boss away and enjoys an excellent work environment. Tread carefully, though. Fail to ensure your treasure gets what they need and you're on a hiding to hard work.

Really top-notch loafing requires teamwork: the team does the work, you do the loafing. The key to that is making sure that the people who actually work closest to you see that it's in their interest to protect you. To do that you're going to have to weave that magic charm on them, let them know you're on their side, and that you have the key to their future happiness. If you don't have a hope in hell of pulling that one off, then it's equally effective (though harder to achieve) to let them know that you have the key to their very best skeleton closets. Since the best skeletons tend to be hidden safely beyond the reach of the full-time layabout, then the first option is the best and that means that you will have to put a bit of effort into getting your staff grades, salaries and perks above the norm. A team in line is half the job done.

Truly accomplished slackers then ensure that they spend a vast amount of time with clients/on the road/etc. to explain their prolonged absence. Team building, client relationships and marketing are good bets for spending days out of the building without anyone expecting you to have anything to show for it.

One other word of advice: for every top-drawer loafer, there is a nemesis, usually in the form of an ambitious colleague eager to get on, possibly at your expense. This inspires panic in substandard slackers. However, the fact is that the average ambitious middle manager spends less than two years in the same job so if you've got it sweet then don't move on and start again; instead, sit tight and look to your team, not to your new threat.

Defining idea

'If you get to be thirty-five and your job still involves wearing a name tag, you've probably made a serious vocational error.'
DENNIS MILLER, US football coach

7. How do I look?

Like it or not, your appearance and your health are of more and more interest to your employer.

Are you fit for the job?

If your boss is a fitness freak you have a choice of two courses of action. Either you can join your boss and beat the hell out of your colleagues at squash or tennis or whatever, or you can religiously avoid exercise of all sorts. The latter makes a definite point, so think about it.

Nowadays there are myriad ways of keeping fit by working out before or after office hours. If you're a bit anti-exercise, which you probably are (as many of us are), then look carefully at all the opportunities. You don't have to do circuit training on a daily basis to give the impression that your health is as important to you as it is to your company. Walking can do it; so can cycling, jogging or roller-skating. If, however, your only exercise is straining to get the cork out of the bottle and the occasional one-night

Here's an idea for you...

It is never a good idea in career terms to fail at anything, so don't try and do too much. For example, try using a personal trainer just once a week or twice a month. That should spur you to some effort. It will eventually be embarrassing to tell them week after week that you haven't been off the sofa since you last met.

stand, you could follow nutritionist
Nigel Bentley's advice and get off
the bus or the tube a few stops early
and walk the rest of the way.

If there are sports facilities at work
use them by all means, but don't
make a big thing about it. A lot of
people, maybe most people, eventually find doing gym exercises
monotonous and boring. So don't make yourself a hostage to fortune
by sounding off about going to the gym every day after work; your
bosses will notice when you stop.

Defining idea

'This is the law of the Yukon, that
only the strong shall thrive;
That surely the Weak shall perish, and
only the fit survive.'
ROBERT W. SERVICE, Canadian poet

What do your clothes say?

A trainer worked with a senior telecommunications person, and his
advice is not for the faint-hearted. He says that you should avoid
looking like everyone else. He always wore eccentric clothes – green
corduroy suits featured heavily, along with brightly coloured braces
and ties. In the nature of the course the trainer had to ask the question
'What do you think your clothes say about you?' The telecoms guy
responded, 'They say that although I have got a senior job in your
organisation, you will never own me.' If the first thing board members
know about you is that you wear yellow suits, you have made your
point. Some of them may not like it, but this is compensated for by the
fact that they've noticed you. The right question to ask yourself is
whether your clothes are saying what you want them to say.

27

8. Back the right horse

You need to get noticed. Identify who is important to your progress, and get to them. Sometimes that will mean bypassing a human blockage.

Suppose, for example, that your job is to supply computer and telecommunications solutions to the finance department of a company. Your customer and decision maker is the Finance Director, but on a day-to-day basis there will be a key person whom you meet regularly and with whom you form plans for future approval by the Finance Director. Such people can usually be divided into three categories – the Good, the Bad and the Ugly.

Here's an idea for you...

Never ask Mr Bad for permission to go and see the decision maker. If he refuses (which he probably will), you're then in an impossible situation. If you go behind his back, then you're heading for a confrontation and the relationship will be ruined for good. No – do it first and beg forgiveness later.

The Good are terrific to work with. They understand their business and they are happy to tell you all about it, so that you can come up with the best possible plan together. Cultivate such people. Help them to enhance their reputations and they will help you enhance yours. They will probably be quite happy for you to talk to the ultimate decision maker should you need to, but they'll do it with you as part of the team.

The Bad are often bad because they are scared. They're scared of their boss, they're scared of making mistakes and they're probably scared of a brilliant careerist like you. They probably don't know enough about their business to really brief you on what it is they want and will probably bar you from seeing the decision maker until you have earned their trust. To do this achieve some good, high-profile results that end up on the Finance Director's desk, and make sure Mr Bad gets all the credit.

At the point when he trusts you, Mr Bad should let you meet his boss. There is a problem if he won't. Access to his Director is vital if you are to carry out your role. So, like it or not, you have to get to them. Once you have created a relationship with his boss, Mr Bad will never be in such a strong position again to get in your way.

Now for the Ugly. Mr Ugly is mean. He doesn't trust you, he doesn't trust his boss, he doesn't trust anyone. Quite often such people are bullies. You can't really play along with them if they are not allowing you to do the best you can for your customer; so you have to grasp the nettle and probably cause a major stink. The way to deal with them is to cause them some fear, uncertainty and doubt.

Defining idea

'The significant problems that we face cannot be solved by the same level of thinking that created them.'
ALBERT EINSTEIN

9. Show me the money

Test your market value.

How can you find out if you're underpaid or overpaid? And what can you do about it? When you buy something for quite a bit less than you expected, you've got a bargain. When your employers pay you less than your market worth, they've got a bargain and the chances are you're being ripped off.

Here's an idea for you...

Compile a table of all the elements you'd like to see in your salary package and then use that as a basis to compare offers. The salary packages that companies offer these days are sophisticated affairs. A particularly good pension scheme, perhaps coupled with other benefits and perks, might mean that the company offering the lower salary could be offering the better package.

So here's a question: are your employers showing you enough money?

If you've only just joined a new company, then the chances are you've had an opportunity to negotiate with them and you've ended up getting the going market rate. If you've been with the company for years and years, then your salary should at least have risen to the company's maximum pay for your grade. That might not be your market rate – for example, if you work in a lower-paying sector – but it probably won't be too bad a deal.

You may be at risk if you've been with a company for a reasonable but not a very long time. Have you been in your current job for 3–10 years? If so, you may find that you're being paid less than your more experienced work colleagues (not unreasonably, perhaps). However, you may also find that recent starters are either being paid more than you or are at least snapping at your heels salary-wise.

Most employers have to pay at or close to the market rate to buy in new people. Rather fewer employers pay at or close to the prevailing market rate to retain good people. Once you're in the company pay system, your pay increases tend to be linked to the level of inflation and across-the-board, company-wide pay deals. Not all company pay systems are fluid and flexible enough to recognise what is going on in your specific job sector.

If you are not convinced that you are being paid the rate for the job, it's worth researching your market value before your next salary review so that you can make the case for what you believe you deserve.

Defining idea

'People who earn a lot of money are not necessarily more clever or more highly qualified than people who earn very little money. People who earn a lot of money...have a higher self-concept level of income.'
RICHARD DOBBINS and **BARRIE O. PETTMAN**, *What Self-made Millionaires Really Think, Know and Do!*

10. Nothing fails like success

Every great idea contains seeds of its own failure.

In the Greek sporting games of ancient times the eventual victor was crowned with a laurel wreath. But if the winner wanted to remain a champion, he could not afford to 'rest on his laurels'. Even maintaining the same standard won't be enough to guarantee victory next time. The world moves on, standards improve, and your competition overhauls you. Charles Darwin expressed this principle starkly; in effect, he said, if you can't evolve more quickly than your environment, then you're doomed.

Here's an idea for you...

Sit down and list your winning life strategies. Think about things like how you gain new friends, how you tackle exams, how you have succeeded in your career and so on – you may well find that you have recurring patterns that you deploy. Then consider how 'future-proof' these strategies are.

According to business writer Richard Pascale, even if we manage to locate the formula for company success, it will be a formula with a sell-by date. He summed this phenomenon up with a memorable phrase: nothing fails like success.

Success has such a short shelf-life these days that the very factors that bring us success today contain the seeds of our destruction tomorrow. So the challenge for each of us is

Defining idea

'Imitation is suicide.'
RALPH WALDO EMERSON

not to lapse into complacency when we achieve a level of success. Rather we need to develop a sense of 'divine discontent' – by all means recognising and revelling in our achievements but also constantly striving to make the next leap forward.

Here are two key questions to think about:
Taking in all aspects of your life, what is working for you now perfectly well, that you know in your heart of hearts won't work anything like as well in one year's time?
This could be about your job, your relationships, your financial situation, the qualifications you currently hold, the level of knowledge you have about a particular subject, your current level of fitness and so on. It could even be about something as down to earth as the state of your car, your sash windows or your computer. Be as thorough and as comprehensive as you can.

What do you need to do about the areas you've identified and when do you need to act?
Having determined those areas of your life where a 'more of the same' strategy just won't deliver the goods, put together some form

of action plan setting out when and how you plan to deal with the problem. A word of advice, though – think about how you ensure that you keep your plans away from the gaze of those people you wouldn't want to know what you have written.

11. You are totally responsible for you

It's a great mistake to think that anyone is as interested in your career as you are.

Even if you have a very open relationship with your boss the annual appraisal is vital to your career plan. Do the preparation and preferably do it better than your boss. Get yourself ready and in the right frame of mind by asking yourself these questions:

■ What value have you added to your job?
■ Where is it that you would like to go?
■ What do you need to do to get there?
■ Why should your boss support these plans? What's in it for them?

Answering these questions before an appraisal interview will mean that you will make the most productive use of this great opportunity to talk about yourself. If you've got a clear idea of your career strategy you'll be much more impressive than an employee who agrees to whatever is suggested and has no proposals of his or her own. More or less writing your own appraisal should make life easier for your boss as well.

You need to be able to prove that you are a valuable asset to the organisation and that if it invests in you, you will become even more valuable. Start from the very top. What words can you use that link your activities with the fundamental vision or mission of the organisation you work for? Then come down through the division and eventually to your boss.

Here's an idea for you...

Lots of managers like to broadcast the fact that they don't really take the appraisal system seriously, that they have done no prep and that the whole thing will be over in twenty minutes. Encourage this thinking, agree that it's a ritual and that only the salary review has any significance. And then go home and do the preparation assiduously.

Another key thing to remember at appraisal time is that the person interviewing you is not an unidentifiable member of the corporate zoo but a person with ambitions and career plans. Be sensitive to this; you are trying to get your boss to adopt your plan. A little flattery can go a long way.

You may already have a job purpose statement or description agreed with your employer. If not, the appraisal is a splendid opportunity to define your own. If you already have a job purpose statement, expand on it to ensure that your future career aspirations are as easy as possible to achieve.

12. Magnum opus

Creating a business plan is like bearing your soul to the world.

A great business plan is really simple. No matter how complex your business, the business plan should give any reader, no matter what their background, a huge insight into the business, your market, your goals and an insight into how you intend to succeed.

In terms of length it need only be as long as it takes to explain the proposition. Don't set yourself a page count and work towards that – write the plan, and if anything try and edit it down to 75% of the original size. A very long document will just bore people and might convince them that you are hiding insecurities behind reams of stats, figures and a few poems thrown in for light relief. Nor is it a marketing document comprising only forward-looking statements that will be nigh on impossible to achieve. It's a working document, one that a good business refers to again and again.

Business plans really do reveal all, namely your own company's strengths and weaknesses, and are highly confidential documents that are not for public consumption. Be careful who gets to see it and understand fully why a certain person needs to see it. Be sure to number each version and destroy older versions so that confusion does not arise.

What readers are looking for in a
business plan is to be taken on a
journey, from start to finish, of how
you are going to make this business
work. Acknowledge the
competition and show categorically
that you have researched the
market. List your competitor's
strengths and weaknesses. If you are

able to obtain financial data (try the annual shareholder reports), quote
this and show where your business fits into the market.

When planning how you are going to tackle the marketing aspect of
the business, don't just list what you intend to do, work out a timeline
(for yourself more than for others) and give people a point of reference
of when certain projects or campaigns will begin and how long they
will last. Break down the costs for each individual campaign and explain
the rationale behind the expenditure and timing.

When the plan is complete you will need to test it on someone you
trust but who is not involved in the business or the same industry. Can
it be read and understood by someone completely removed from the
business? Whatever terminology or areas they find difficult to
understand must be revised or explained – your plan must have
universal appeal.

Once complete and fully edited it is time to make sure that the plan itself is well presented. Having the document bound, or at least placed in a colour co-ordinated folder will make you and your proposal all the more attractive – readers are also less likely to lose random pages, which helps too.

13. What's my line?

Your career depends on your organisation meeting its objectives, and on you being seen as making a big contribution to those aims.

The word 'strategy' is possibly the most ill-used piece of management-speak in the business. Middle managers often complain that their board of directors doesn't have a strategy. This is normally not the case. The board's strategy may be wrong but it does have one. Maybe middle management has not been told about it or maybe they have misunderstood it. It is, in fact, a crucial function of the board to plan and implement a strategy, so you need a reputation as a strategic thinker to get to the top. Start working on that now.

Here's an idea for you...

Get yourself a good definition of the strategy of any staff departments that are important to you. The marketing department is a good place to start – after all, they are responsible for agreeing the top-level strategy of what you are going to sell and to whom.

Come down a few levels to team leaders and the accusation that they don't have a strategy can look truer. It is difficult for them to have an up-to-date strategy, particularly in organisations that do not give concrete guidelines on what a strategy is and how and when to review it. Difficulties abound:

Defining idea

'A strategy is no good unless people fundamentally believe in it.'
ROBERT HASS, businessman

- It is difficult for a team leader to build a strategy because it takes time.
- Short-term pressures stop the team getting on with the job of creating a strategy and even when it does, the strategy is frequently ignored whenever a customer or other significant pressure blows it off course.
- Your best strategy may be impossible because other parts of the business will not change to suit you.
- Building a team strategy needs consensus, so some team members are going to have to compromise – never easy.

But if it's difficult it must be an area where the ambitious manager can build some career points. Put simply, you need to build a strategy with your team, agree it with all your main stakeholders or interested parties, including your customers, and flaunt it. You've got to know the organisation's strategy before you start. Keeping it simple, what is it?

In an ideal world, a strategy is a plan of what an organisation is going to sell to which markets and how. The strategic plan allows everyone to know how they should do their jobs, what the boundaries are and how the board will appraise any suggestions for doing new things. It is the strategy's job to bring focus to everyone's work. You must get to know it in terms that are not business-school babble.

14. Doing nothing at work – employees

The key to loafing is to create an illusion of purpose and industry that deflects the scrutiny of superiors.

The key points to loafing are as true today as they ever were. The first is that if you want to spend all day doing nothing then you'd better have a cover story. The second is that whatever that story is you must be prepared to launch into it with conviction and the kind of enthusiasm that suggests nothing would please you more than to explain it in incomprehensible detail until your interrogator's ears bleed. Today's loafers also have at their fingertips an armoury of high-tech tools to use as props.

Once the great trick was to always be seen with a clipboard. Clipboards speak volumes about business, importance, and those endless 'jobs' like 'stocktaking' and 'time and motion studies' that were always nothing more than the inventions of loafers. The trusty clipboard can still come in handy but if you really want to get away with it these days it's time to go digital.

Here's an idea for you...

Get yourself a key friend in geekdom. Someone savvy on the systems side is needed to tell you crucial info such as whether the company has keystroke monitoring systems to record effort and detect games players. Bunking off to see a systems person is also a universally accepted ploy.

Digital devices add a whole new dimension to loafing because their very presence intimidates the Luddites, and their multi-tasking flexibility makes it hard for even the initiate to call your bluff. Proof positive of this is the evolution of the uber-loafer – the king of the freeloading food chain. Posing as 'systems administrator', 'network engineer' or any one of a dozen similarly meaningless monikers, these geek gods have reached the noodling nirvana where they can face down anybody from line managers to the CEO. This is done with nothing more than a withering look and a sarcastic outpouring of gobbledygeek.

You don't have to be one to take a leaf from their book. Even the humblest warehouse worker, if wielding one of those brilliant, handheld data input devices, is in a position of strength because

Defining idea

'Look at me: I worked my way up from nothing to a state of extreme poverty.'
GROUCHO MARX

nobody, not even the person who bought them, really knows all the things you might be doing with them. Other examples include BlackBerries ('of course I'm not skiing; can't you see I'm emailing?'), laptops ('Fragfest? All-out Hover Tank war? Certainly not; it's a 3D graphic representation of next-year's projected margins'), or any kind of spreadsheet (make sure you can bring up an elaborate diagrammatic representation with a triumphant punch of the button).

15. Please find attached...

A top-notch covering letter can be viewed as either essential or totally unnecessary and we've no way of knowing which is the case.

In terms of how the covering letter is regarded nowadays, there are two distinct camps in the recruiters' world. In one camp are those recruiters who bin accompanying letters on sight because they

42

expect applicants to make their case entirely through their CV. They assume that people will produce a customised CV and that therefore an accompanying letter is simply a lingering nod to a piece of outmoded social etiquette. Spend forty minutes carefully crafting a bespoke letter in these cases and it'll be a waste of time as its unlikely to make any difference to the recruiter's decision about whether or not you deserve an interview.

Here's an idea for you...

Always find a named person to write to. Anything addressed to 'The Personnel Manager' or opening with 'Dear Sir/Madam' is liable to end up on the desk of an admin underling. If, on the other hand, you write to an individual personally, you'll turn the epistolary equivalent of a cold call into a much warmer approach.

In the second camp, there are just as many recruiters who expect to see a covering letter that sets out a full and convincing argument why the writer should be pencilled in for an interview. In these cases, the absence of a covering letter would do your cause real harm.

Since we rarely know which of these two camps we're likely to be dealing with the safest bet for the prudent job-hunter is to write a covering letter on the basis that it just might make a difference.

Your covering letter should obviously be typed, regardless of how neat your handwriting is. And regarding the content of a covering letter, the structure can be broken down into three sections:

1. **Make the connection.** Explain why you're writing at this particular time. If it's in response to an advertisement, identify where you saw the ad and when it appeared (this can help recruiters to identify which papers or magazines bring in the best response). If your approach is speculative, still try to give a compelling reason why you're interested in that particular company.

2. **Make your pitch.** Describe what you can offer the company. Try to make sure that every point you make is likely to be relevant to their needs.

3. **Describe what's coming next.** Take control of the process by saying what you want to happen next. Perhaps say something like, 'I'll call you in a week's time to see if there might be value in our meeting up' or a less pushy 'I look forward to hearing from you.' Follow up with a telephone call if you've heard nothing after ten days or so.

16. Ready, aim, fire

Keeping someone in your team who plainly is not going to make it can be very bad for your career.

When it comes to sacking somebody timing is vital; but equally important is how you do it. You come across people whom you served as a customer, or for whom you worked, frequently enough for you to want to ensure that you only make enemies when there is no alternative. You may also come across people who worked for you in an earlier life, which means, of course, that you may come across people whom you fired.

Here are the dos and don'ts of sacking:

■ Do prepare carefully, not only for the meeting but also for what will happen in personnel terms after it.

■ Don't let the firee talk you out of it. If you've made your decision, stick to it. You will never recover with this person if you change your mind.

■ Do have a stiff drink before the meeting. You need to look

Here's an idea for you...

Sometimes the Human Resources rules cause a hold-up. HR is, of course, quite right to protect the company's position and make sure that you do nothing that would prejudice that. But if the delay is going to cause problems, argue strongly that the company should buy its way out of it.

Defining idea

'Never flinch – make up your own
mind and do it.'
MARGARET THATCHER

assertive, firm and friendly, not a
nervous wreck.

■ Don't relax too much. Jokes might
not go down too well right now.

■ Do give a generous if not lavish
settlement.

■ Do go through the process meticulously. It is important that it's you
who gives the generous settlement, not an industrial tribunal.

Now's the time to consider the value of headhunters to your career.
Headhunters are something else you should spend the organisation's
money lavishly on – they have an encyclopaedic knowledge of your
industry and the people and opportunities in it. Perhaps you could
help the person you are firing meet with a headhunter you know. That
can sugar the pill. At the same time, encourage the headhunters to
make suggestions to you at any time, not just when you want people
or want a job for someone else. That way you are also encouraging
them to do the same in terms of job opportunities for you.

Be very careful of the current fad for 'head-shunting'. This avoids the
painful process of sacking someone by getting a headhunter to place
them with another company. In theory, you avoid the expense of
severance pay, and remove any threat of being sued for wrongful
dismissal. However, someone who discovers that the ploy has been
visited on them can still sue for unfair dismissal, and if the receiving
company believes it has been duped, it also might have a case.

17. Brass tacks

Part of any interview will involve a somewhat technical discussion about the nitty-gritty of the job you're applying for. Make sure you get the detail right for your audience.

You've got to say enough, of course, to prove that you have the technical ability to do the job. But leave any detail about that until after you've presented the answer in a way that shows the bridge between what your function is and how the organisation succeeds. Say you've been asked how you'd go about managing a project.

A project, or anything come to that, has its internal issues. You have to get the team to carry out the function and meet its objectives. But what outside managers are interested in is the interface where the project contributes to or harms the success of the organisation. They're also interested in the project when it impacts on other

Here's an idea for you...

Work out how to explain your job in 100 words. You've got to explain it in a way that shows that you have a wealth of knowledge behind this statement which makes you a reliable resource to get the job done. Try it out on a few people. Teenagers are a good bet, since you can measure their concentration span in nanoseconds. When you've made that work, reduce it to fifty words.

parts of the organisation. These are the bridges you're looking for; they're the 'benefits' your function brings to the party.

So, 'At the outset I develop the objectives of the project and spend whatever time it takes to get all the stakeholders' agreement that we've got them right' is much better than 'While not a perfect critical path analysis engine, Microsoft Project can be used to control the project and it has the benefit that most people are used to using it...'

Similarly, 'I'd talk to as many managers with relevant experience as possible to work out the resources we'd need during the project' is much better than 'Once you've got the action plan the resource plan is quite straightforward. All you have to do is to reproduce the action plan as a resource plan.'

Your qualifications, training and experience of doing the job make it a whole lot easier to spend time on this bit than on tricky questions about subjects such as managing difficult people. Another useful technique to keep things simple is to give them the simplest possible explanation and then ask them if they want more detail.

18. Did someone say something?

Better your communication skills and enhance your performance at work.

The real skill in communicating is how well we listen. We'd all like to be sure that we're making the best decisions possible in all aspects of our lives. But unless we listen to people, we won't fully understand what they're saying. Often, when we probably don't have the full picture, we leap ahead and make a decision, and then spend an enormous amount of time sorting out the problems we've helped to create. Remember the disasters with the space shuttles *Columbia* and *Challenger*? The overall conclusion was that the accidents should never have happened because there were people further down the organisation who realised what the problems were. However, nobody was listening to them.

Imagine that you're walking towards a beautiful castle. You can't see the castle clearly because

Here's an idea for you...

At your next meeting, listen to people and don't interrupt. Observe what's happening. How much real listening is going on? What opportunities are being missed due to interruptions? How many people can't get a word in edgeways? Whose ideas are being driven through? What changes can be made to achieve better outcomes?

Defining idea

*'The reason we have two ears and
only one mouth is that we may listen
the more and talk the less.'*
ZENO, Greek philosopher

it's hidden by mist, but you know
you really want to get there and
explore it. While you're walking,
you meet a large group of people
who knock you over, trample all
over you and kick you. Once
they've gone, you get up and start
heading towards the castle again. Soon you meet two great friends
who persuade you to go with them on another path before you go
to the castle. You enjoy your trip but then return to the path to
where you wanted to go in the first place – the castle. Next, you
meet someone who knows exactly where you're going and doesn't
want you to get there. That person becomes violent and eventually
drags you off to somewhere else.

Now imagine this scenario. You're in a meeting and you have an
idea that isn't totally clear but you want to share it, nevertheless.
However, every time you try to open your mouth you find that
everyone else is so busy talking about their ideas that you can't get a
word in edgeways. Or they want you to look at their ideas first. Or
you're told that your idea can't be considered because a decision has
already been made. What is the difference between these two
pictures? There isn't one, really. Every time you interrupt someone
else it is, in fact, mental violence.

19. Be organised

How can you be sure that you're going to end the day having really *done* something?

Don't be fooled by the latest newfangled time-management kit and associated manuals that will ultimately do you no good. You only need one device: the good old-fashioned to-do list.

Whatever you use to create your to-do list you need to concentrate on three things:

■ smart and realistic prioritisation of the tasks
■ the breaking down of big tasks into smaller, more achievable ones
■ the making of a new list for every new day.

When it comes to prioritising, remember the '80/20 rule': 80% of results come from 20% of efforts. This means that roughly one in five of the items on your list are truly essential and you should concentrate on completing these. Everything else may be useful, but the world won't end if they don't get done.

Here's an idea for you...

Write a list of impossible tasks. Put it away somewhere safe and only get it out at the end of a day if you're completely overwhelmed, or you feel you haven't really achieved what you set out to do. Looking at it might help you regain a sense of perspective and become re-energised for tomorrow.

Defining idea...

'Failing to plan is a plan to fail.'
EFFIE JONES

Don't confine yourself to simple A, B, C-style rankings of importance, however: you also need to recognise that some tasks take longer than others. For example, one 'A' category phone call might take just five minutes while an equivalent writing task could take as much as five hours. If you have one big important thing that needs to be done by the end of the day, then be aware that a dozen smaller tasks are hidden within that one bald statement. Each one of these smaller tasks needs to be itemised and allocated time. If you don't do this, how can you ever be sure that your one big to-do item of the day is really achievable?

To combat a cluttered list, make two separate lists: one of things you absolutely must do today and another of things you might get round to if you have the time or inclination. Don't even think about looking at the second list until the first has been dealt with.

Compile your lists for tomorrow at the end of each working day. Don't wait until morning and find that the first task on your new to-do list is writing a to-do list. And don't just re-edit today's list – start afresh each time. Quite often people use up the last half hour of their working day tidying up and 'clearing the decks' for the next day. Don't. It's much better to greet the new day with a messy desk and a clear head than the other way round.

20. Leave on time

Reduce interruptions. Reclaim your evenings. Take control.

The secret is to have your goals clear in your mind. Think weekly, then daily; see the big picture. Decide what you want to have done by Friday and then break each goal into smaller tasks that have to be undertaken to achieve all you want by Friday. Slot these tasks in throughout your week. This helps you prioritise, so that the tricky and difficult things, or tasks that depend on other people's input, don't sink to the bottom. It also means you are giving attention to all that you have to do and not spending too much time on one task at the beginning of the week. Concentrate on three or four items on your 'to-do' list at once. You won't be overwhelmed.

If your job demands creativity, block out your most creative periods so that you can concentrate on your projects. Don't allow them to be impinged upon by meetings and phone calls that could be done any time. Here are some other ideas.

- **Make the phone call you're dreading.** That call that saps your energy all day. Just do it.

Here's an idea for you...

When you're an administrative lynchpin, set up a shared file where people can go to find the information or resources they'd usually get from you without interrupting you.

Defining idea...

■ **Have meetings in the morning.** People want to whizz through stuff and get on with their day. Morning meetings go much faster.

■ **Check emails three times a day.** First thing in the morning, just after lunch and just before you leave are ideal times. Then you don't use email as a distraction.

■ **Limit phone calls.** Talk to other people when it suits you, not them. Limit your calls as you do your emails – to three times a day. Make a list of calls you have to make that day. Call first thing. If someone isn't there, leave a message and unless you have to talk to them urgently, ask them to call you back at your next 'phone period'. Just before lunch and around 4:30 are good. That means neither of you will linger over the call. Most of us have some control over incoming calls: very politely say 'Sorry, I'm in the middle of something,' tell the caller when you'll be free and most people will offer to call back. Social chat is important and nice but most of us spend too much time on it. Time restrictions stop us rambling on.

21. Changing horses mid-career

If you make a move to a new company your fellow managers there have an advantage over you...

They know the ropes and how to shine in the existing environment. It is therefore a very good idea to do something early on to question that environment and change it in a high-profile way.

If you are joining at a fairly high level it is likely that the people who hired you saw you as an agent of change, for a part of their business or culture which is underperforming. If this is the case, you can afford to take a few risks in the early days.

Take this example: A manager moved from one company to another much larger and longer-established one. He knew that senior management were implementing a huge programme

Here's an idea for you...

If you are staying in your organisation have a long, hard think about change. What really needs to be changed? Think deeply and don't be held back by things that seem to be cast in stone – nothing is. If the change is within your authority, just do it. If it's not, go to the person who *could* do it and persuade them to let you do it.

Defining idea...

of change aimed at knocking the old-fashioned corners off those managers who had served with the organisation since the year dot.

Many of these people were accustomed to a culture where seniority counted highly. They were also struggling with the idea that the customer was king. On his very first day the new manager took action using the car park as his agent. He removed every parking space allocated on the basis of management seniority, and reallocated the best spaces to customers only. As he was doing this he realised that some areas were not only dark but also outside the range of the security cameras.

So he allocated the next best spaces nearest to the entrance to those women who sometimes or regularly worked late. At a stroke he got the support of those people who felt held back by the old guard, and of the more ambitious women willing to work long hours. His action also became high-profile without his having to tell a soul – the old guard did it for him. They were fuming. They sent angry emails to the HR department and senior managers in all parts of the organisation complaining about this loss of their hard-earned privilege. By the end of his very first day he had a very high profile.

He had sorted the resisters to change from the enthusiasts for it, and impressed on senior management his grasp of what they were looking for in terms of cultural change. Senior management congratulated themselves, modestly of course, for hiring the right person for the job.

22. Persuasion

What's the most effective way of influencing people?

When we want people to follow our lead, we usually try to find as many different ways to get our thoughts across as possible. If someone disagrees, we just try to come at it another way. However, does this actually work?

When you give someone a problem to solve they'll begin to think it through and pathways or traces will be created through the brain. You tell them you think they've got it wrong and they need to think it through again. This they

Here's an idea for you...

For the duration of your very next conversation try not to use the word 'I'. Concentrate entirely on 'you'. Ask 'you' questions. What do you think about this? How might you handle this? This way you'll see how much more people are able to contribute. You'll also notice how difficult you'll find it to not take over and voice your ideas.

do and they may possibly find a new pathway but it's highly likely that they'll go down the same pathway, making that idea deeper or more firmly entrenched. Ask them to think it through again and it'll be almost impossible for them to come up with a new solution. It's not that they don't want to, it's just that the pathways have now been created and the brain finds it virtually impossible to move away from those pathways.

When you look at this picture it's obvious that continually trying to change someone's mind by telling them, yet again, why you think the way you do, is likely to be less than useless.

Most of us think that we're open to ideas, that we are caring to others and that we encourage them to come forward with their thoughts and suggestions. But this is not usually the case. Without even realising it, we usually communicate by giving our point of view, giving our suggestions and telling people why we don't agree with their ideas.

What we don't do is support their ideas, ask for their opinions, test our understanding of what they're saying, summarise all their points of view, or take their ideas and demonstrate their value by building on them. We don't invite them into the conversation.

Actually, if you really want to influence people the knack is to ask questions that allow them the opportunity to think about something in a different way. In other words, allow the brain to come from a different start point. First, focus on helping them explore their idea. Then focus on developing their idea to incorporate your own.

23. Detox your CV

You don't get two chances to make a first impression, so remove any harmful content from your CV that might raise negative thoughts.

Part of creating an impressive CV is about only including information that will make a positive impact on the employer. The reverse side of that particular coin is to excise any information that is likely to impact on the employer negatively.

Strip out surplus content

Sometimes knowing what to cut out of your CV is a matter of common sense, but sometimes it's more of a judgement call.

In the common-sense category comes all the gratuitous information, information you've not been asked explicitly to provide that is likely to do your cause more harm than good if you include it. For

Here's an idea for you...

Use spellcheck, but remember it won't catch every error. An unnerving example is that if you left the 'l' out of 'public relations', spellcheck would happily nod that through, but the PR Director with the vacancy might be less forgiving!

example, an obsession with extreme sports might keep your adrenalin high, but it'll probably cause employers a frisson of concern. Likewise, mentioning the penalty points you have on your driving licence can only have a negative impact. Or listing your personal website if it happens to contain pictures of you mooning in Falaraki.

In the judgement-call terrain, matters aren't quite so clear-cut. It's more about tone and nuance. Imagine you're applying for a role that's 100% about dealing with customers face to face. Describing the face-to-face element of your current role ought, therefore, to get the recruiter's interest. If you devote, say, two bullet points out of four to this facet of your job, it will come over as a substantive part of what you do. However, if those two bullets are out of eight, you're diluting their impact. Should you place the two bullets in the middle or towards the bottom of the eight, then that will diminish their effect further.

Clean up spelling errors

Employers have a habit of assuming that anybody who makes a spelling mistake in their CV is likely to make mistakes on the job. At the very least, you're guilty of a lack of attention to detail. The

following bloopers were taken
from real CVs and covering letters:

■ Special skills: Thyping.
■ Objection: To utilise my skills in
sales.
■ I am a rabid typist.

Defining idea...

*'The key to any game is to use your
strengths and hide your weaknesses.'*
**PAUL WESTPHAL, former basketball
player**

Detox your quirky individuality
No photo, no wacky fonts, no coloured paper, no jokes, no eccentric
hobbies, no exclamation marks, no personal pronouns, no
'Curriculum Vitae' at the top of each page, no volunteered salary
details, no mention of political affiliation, no early schooling details
and no unnecessary repetition of facts.

24. Facing the inevitable question

**You know it's going to come up: 'So, why
do you want this job?'**

It should be reasonably easy to answer this as long as you're going
for the right job. If it's very difficult, then ask yourself if this is the

Here's an idea for you...

The best way to prepare is to find someone to role-play the interviewer and then try out with them the actual words you're going to use when dealing with this one. If you can get someone in the same industry that would be best, but anyone with good experience of organisations or business should be able to help.

right employer for you before you go in. An employer wants people to join them with enthusiasm for the challenges they're about to face. Similarly you want to get into an environment where your working life gives you joy rather than grief. Research and good self-insight will give you the right answer to achieve both aims.

What's in it for you?

It's probably best to start the dual answer with the straightforward answer to the question. So do your research and reply in terms of the company's attributes as you find them. Whatever the situation is; you can still paint it as ideal for you. 'Most people want to work for the market leader; I could use your name with pride' could equally be 'I like the way you've made such progress in your industry'.

Now try to get in something about their reputation. 'I understand that you can offer me a stable, challenging and inspiring work environment – you certainly have that reputation. I think it's the sort of environment that brings out the best in me.'

Then compliment the company on what it actually does. 'Many people regard your products and services as the best around. I like to work for someone who is passionate about service and quality.'

What's in it for them?

Try to work out a way of illustrating that everything you've done points at you being the right person for

them. Perhaps start from specific experience. Imagine you're a team leader in credit control: 'My experience in the credit control department of a builders' merchants was, frankly, like a tough school. The building industry is always suffering from companies going under. I know about collection periods, credit ratings calculated from company reports and I've heard every excuse under the sun for not being able to pay. I think I'd be able to help others to learn from that experience.'

Now relate the specific skills to the goals of the organisation. 'I understand the benefits to you of getting payment in on time or even before time; I've controlled cash flow and seen the impact it can have on profitability.'

You can also be more open about your skills where you're sure they're appropriate, and something more personal can emphasise your uniqueness. Then bring everything together: 'So you see why I was excited when I saw your job ad; you seem to need a person with pretty much the experience, skills and interests that I've developed.'

25. Get your own way with a consultant

External consultants present both an opportunity and a threat to your career. Exploit the opportunity and avoid the threat by planning how and when to get involved with them.

Since the turn of the century the consultancy world has dealt with many problems – a dramatic fall in demand, scandals such as Enron and customers who feel that they were ripped off and deceived by consultants in the past. Daily rates have plummeted. At the same time many new consultants have set up shop. Many of these new freelancers were made redundant, especially from the large consultancies. They believe themselves to have many skills covering all aspects of business life. Few of them have many clients.

So the stage is set for the career person to cash in. Consultants cost less than they used to; so you can get flashier ones for the same price. They are hungry for work and they will tend to remember the people who hire them. Arm

Here's an idea for you...

Is there a tricky issue where you're finding it hard to get your own way? Could an outside consultant help? If so, ensure the case for bringing in a consultant is well made.

yourself with the essential
information:

■ What is the purpose of hiring a
consultant?
■ What can an outside agency do
that internal staff cannot?
■ Can you justify the cost?

Defining idea...

*'Here's the rule for bargains: "Do
other men for they would do you."
That's the true business concept.'*
CHARLES DICKENS, *Martin Chuzzlewit*

Now brief the consultant extremely carefully so that the answer
they come up with is exactly what you first thought of.

You can use a consultant for career benefits. As you know, one of the
major issues that you have to deal with is company politics, the
messy stuff that gets in the way of getting a job done. It is inevitable
once you add the unpredictable element of people into any
situation. You can use an outside consultancy firm to provide an
unbiased view to the powers that be. Their opinion may be more
readily accepted than if it was something you'd come up with. And
then there is always the added bonus that external advisers can take
the blame for unpopular but necessary solutions to problems. Your
reputation can stay intact.

Using consultants could be a really smart career move. Spend your
company's money lavishly on them – everybody needs a pal. Such
friendships then give rise to new opportunities in different

organisations, because this is a two-way relationship. If a consultant has a client looking for a top person, and you've previously hired them into your current organisation at huge expense, they may very well introduce and recommend you. They need pals too.

26. Cunning plans

Careerists need to treat a fluid list of complex activities as a project. Make sure you don't have one arm tied behind your back before you start.

A lot of projects are doomed to fail before they start because the manager doesn't recognise the need to define and manage activities as a project. Here's the holy trinity of rules for announcing and managing a project:

- The timescale from start to finish is more than a month, often a lot longer.
- There is more than one function involved.
- You do not have direct authority over all the people resources needed.

If these three elements are in place, go to your boss and propose that he or she becomes the sponsor of the project. Outline your vision for how things will look once the project is complete. Make sure the timing is right. Before you announce your project, test for 'management initiative overload'. This is a syndrome that haunts many organisations which have too many initiatives going on simultaneously, none of which ever gets completed. Don't start something that you can't finish. Never fight a battle you can't win. You're going to run it high-profile, so it's got to be successful. If your vision is bold and useful enough your boss may cancel someone else's pet project to divert resources to your new one. This is excellent careermanship, and if it happens, make sure you are the first person to sympathise with the thwarted colleague: '…but what could I do, you know what it's like when X has the bit between her teeth?'

Now, kick-start it by thinking the project through to the end. The key to the beginning of the plan is assessing the chances of success. Look for strong driving forces that, for example, close a competitive gap, or gain a competitive edge. They are strong if they translate easily into sales growth and so on. Restraining forces include people's natural resistance to change and their current workload.

Here's an idea for you…

Find something difficult that needs to be done, some major change that the organisation needs to make. Perhaps your boss hasn't thought of it or has thought it too tough, but he or she would be happy to take the credit for it. Offer to manage it, and deliver.

Remember, most projects aimed at improving the working environment actually create more work for people. Weigh up these forces. If the risk, to business and career, is sensible, go for it.

Then think about roughly the resources you will need and how available those are likely to be. Negotiate for this now, before you volunteer to take on the task.

Finally, check the stakeholders. Make a list of all the people who will in some way be affected by the project – they will not only be your key team members but also your customers and possibly your suppliers. You've got to get them all on board sooner or later, so make sure the list is complete. Think about how much authority your sponsor has, and wriggle out of any project where the sponsor is totally incompetent, or hated sufficiently for people to want anything they touch to fail.

27. Working by the pool

For an ever-growing chunk of the population, working from home isn't a euphemism for skiving; it's a way of life.

For a start, if you have kids under 6 (or 18 if they have a disability) and you have been working for a company for 26 weeks or more then you have the automatic right to apply to work flexibly. The idea is that you then have more time to spend taking care of your kids, but that could mean many things: for example, you could be applying to start work later so as to be able to take the kids to school, or to start earlier and finish earlier so as to be there to pick them up after school. It could also mean working at home a certain number of days a week.

Here's an idea for you...

As part of the flexible working legislation you have the right to take a colleague with you when meeting the boss to discuss your proposal. So instead of reinventing the wheel seek out others in the company who have successfully applied for flexible working and get them on your side.

Employers have a statutory duty to 'consider the applications seriously' and must follow a specific procedure when considering them, which means that they can't refuse you without giving precise reasons. So head them off at the pass by sitting down and putting together a killer application that can't be refused. What you will need to think about is the benefit to the company, not to you.

Try to:
- Explain how you will make up exactly the same time.
- Point out that you will be more motivated and happy with your new timetable, and more productive.

69

- Show that the company may stand to make savings in the office environment.
- Demonstrate that you have the appropriate technology and abilities to do your job from home.
- Consider means of monitoring your performance that can be used to prove you are reaching agreed levels and so back up your claim to be more productive with the new timetable.

Your boss has 28 days from receiving the request to arrange a meeting with you and explore your proposal. Fourteen days after that, the employer must write to you to either agree the new pattern and a start date or else provide clear business grounds as to why your proposal is unworkable. If that's the case, the letter also has to set out the appeal procedure for you to contest the decision. For more details take a look at the DTI website (www.dti.gov.uk).

When you're putting together your proposal bear in mind that you may be setting a precedent and so you are effectively establishing the benefits of flexible working in general. Make doubly sure that you have the facts and figures at your fingertips and can explain how they would affect the company.

An interesting stat to bear in mind is that, according to the Equal Opportunities Commission, 80% of women return to work within 17 months of childbirth, but only 47% return to the same employer. By contrast, employers who offer flexible working patterns have return rates of 90%, saving the business replacement costs and retaining valuable skills and experience. An internal study by BT found that home workers were actually 31% more efficient than their office counterparts.

28. Networking

Exemplary networking is about quality of contacts, not quantity.

Outplacement consultants believe that as many as two-thirds of all job moves come about on the back of networking. As traditional hierarchies have died away and we've become increasingly mobile in our careers, networking is more important than ever.

There are four main types of network: personal, work, professional (e.g. solicitors, accountants, bank managers, shop owners, doctors) and organisations (e.g. professional associations and clubs, chambers of commerce). Here are six tips on how to build and maintain a set of

Here's an idea for you...

Concentrate on getting in touch with a handful of extremely well-connected people. Don't simply go through your contacts resolutely from A to Z. Ask yourself who your 'platinum' contacts are and establish when you're going to get in touch with them.

Defining idea...

'There are four ways, and only four ways, in which we have contact with the world. We are evaluated and classified by these four contacts: what we do, how we look, what we say, and how we say it.'
DALE CARNEGIE

contacts that will open doors:

1. Take the time and effort to build and nurture a network.

There's a book on networking by Harvey Mackay called *Dig Your Well Before You're Thirsty*, which makes the point that you can't make use of a network until you've put one in place, so it makes sense to be constantly developing your contacts.

2. Manage your network on an ongoing basis.

Having somebody's business card tucked away in your desk drawer doesn't necessarily mean that that person is a fully signed up member of your network. Here's the acid test: could you pick up the phone and call them right now without them struggling to remember you or taking umbrage? As a broad rule of thumb, if you haven't had any contact with somebody for at least six months, it may be presumptuous to assume they're part of your network.

3. Be clear about what you're trying to achieve.

The more focused the message you feed into a network, the better the chance that something might come of it. 'I'm looking for a senior project management role in the pharmaceutical industry' is likely to register memorably and positively.

4. Get your network on your side.
Don't antagonise your contacts by seeming to exploit your relationship with them. It's far more effective to ask people if you can tap into their advice and guidance than to look them in the eye and ask them outright for a job.

5. Make use of your network's network.
You can widen your network by using existing contacts to give you the names of other useful people.

6. Keep a record of who you contact and when.
When somebody gives you their business card, jot down on the back of the card where and when you met them.

29. Jump-start your salary

Do you deserve a higher salary? Well, of course you do. Let's look at tactics and techniques for making a persuasive case.

The prerequisites for getting your salary increased are that (a) you are reasonably competent, and (b) you're well regarded by your

Here's an idea for you...

Be flexible. If your boss accepts the validity of your case but pleads emptiness of the piggybank, answer with something like, I can see the problem so let's see what else we can do. Maybe I could have an extra week's holiday and a company car instead.' It is worth bearing in mind that your salary is part of the total package.

employers. Taking these as read, here are some tips for negotiating your way to an optimal package. The first decision you'll have to make is, in the words of Joe Strummer, 'Should I stay or should I go?'

If you decide you want to stay where you are then you'll need to start gathering evidence showing why you deserve an increase. Perhaps you can make the case that colleagues are getting more pay for doing the same work, or that others are getting more money even though you do more work.

Before you fix a time to talk with you boss, make sure you know what you want. This means having three figures in mind: your ideal salary (the most you dare ask for without alienating your boss), your bottom line (the lowest figure you'd settle for) and your realistic goal (the figure that you think you've a good chance of getting).

Armed with this, prepare your case and book a meeting with your boss. Make sure you time this to your best advantage. If you've only been with the company a few months, or if you've just made the mother of all cock-ups, hold off. More precisely, go for a time of day which gives you a chance of finding your boss receptive and in good

humour. When you go to the
meeting, have all the facts and
figures at your fingertips.

If there's nothing doing, don't
despair. Career-wise, it might be an
excellent time to position yourself
for recognition when the money does become available. You can ask
for added responsibilities or a new job title. You're taking a risk, of
course, that you might be working harder in the short term for the
same pay, but you've bolstered your bargaining position. If nothing
comes through eventually, then start looking for a new place to work.

Here are a few tips to deploy when you've been offered a position
with a new company.

- Aim to negotiate with the decision-maker rather than
  intermediaries.
- It's always preferable to negotiate on the basis of a written offer. It
  will help prevent misunderstandings and also depersonalise the
  situation if you are negotiating over a piece of paper.
- Keep the tone positive by reaffirming your real interest in joining
  the company, emphasizing how pleased you were to receive the
  offer – it's just a matter of clearing up a few contractual points.
- Try to give the company a few options; don't box yourself into a
  corner.

Defining idea...

'For they can conquer who believe
they can.'
JOHN DRYDEN

- Don't let the process drag on.

Finally, if you decide to reject the offer, keep it courteous and professional. Remember that the people you are dealing with are probably good networkers; you don't want to be bad-mouthed.

30. Become a core competent

If you want to be smart, build up your knowledge base. Tomorrow's world belongs to the 'core competents'.

Organisations only want us if they perceive us to be a source of added value. So those of us who want to build a substantial career within organisations need to develop for ourselves (and regularly reinvent) a pool of skills and knowledge that will justify our place in a company's shrinking set of vital functions. To put it another way, we need to become one of what writer Stuart Crainer calls the 'Core Competents'.

These are the small number of people in an organisation who are vital to its success. Bill Gates has said that there are 20 people who are pivotal to Microsoft, and that the company would risk bankruptcy or a severe dip in the share price at the very least if they were to leave.

So what sort of steps can we take to build our personal knowledge base and hence increase our worth? Here are a few tips:

- Develop career purpose – people with a vision of the future and goals linked to that vision are far more likely to succeed than others.
- Be visible – find ways to raise your profile.
- Network like crazy.
- Think ahead: taking care of your job is not the same as taking care of your career. To avoid career inertia, schedule in regular reviews of where you and your career is heading.

The crucial thing is never to become complacent about knowledge levels. The skills, knowledge and experience that got us where we are today will not be enough to get us where we might want to be tomorrow. So we need to consciously set out to maintain and build on our current knowledge base, as well as to acquire new skills and knowledge. Then we need to start thinking about what to do when those new skills and knowledge themselves become obsolete.

Here's an idea for you...

Spend time identifying an opportunity that you think will add value to your personal 'brand' in the career marketplace. For example, it might be a job move, getting on board with a high-profile organisational project, joining an organising committee, giving a conference speech, or writing an article for your professional journal – anything that gets your card marked as somebody to watch.

So spend some time thinking about how you can build your personal intellectual capital. Assuming you will need to earn money for a few years yet, what is your game plan for being valued highly in your chosen marketplace in one year's time? How about three years? And five? What do you need to start focusing on now to be where you want to be in the future?

Above all, trust your own judgement. Take regular soundings of other people's views about where the world of work is heading but be sure to make up your own mind. Don't rely on anybody else's view of the future.

31. Dream a little dream

Before putting pen to paper, consider what you want from the work you do.

Here are twelve questions that are designed to help you get a handle on the state of your career. Don't feel you have to answer each question in painstaking detail, simply go for those that seem the most relevant or intriguing.

1. In what elements of your career have you been most successful? And least successful?

2. What aspects of your career have you enjoyed the most? And the least?

3. More specifically, which has been the most satisfying role you have undertaken to date?

Here's an idea for you...

Make a list of the constraints affecting your career choices over the next few years. These may include financial issues, qualifications, where you live and work, your ability to relocate, and so on. After each constraint, make a brief note of the status of that constraint.

4. With the benefit of twenty-twenty hindsight, are there any points in your career or life where you would have made a different choice or decision?

5. How do you feel when you get up to go to work in the morning?

6. What aspects of your current job do you enjoy the most? And the least?

7. Do you enjoy working with others?

8. How are you regarded by the people you work with?

9. Do subordinates, peers and senior managers hold different views about you? If so, what conclusions can you draw from this?

10. Have you had a new boss recently, say, in the last two years? If so, what impact has this had on the way you feel?

11. How ambitious are you?

12. What do you want out of the work you do? Are you getting it?

Unless you're keen to retire, downshift, start your own business or continue as you are, here are your three main career options:

Defining idea...

A new role in the same organisation

Internal career development can be an excellent way of moving into new fields and learning new skills. You wouldn't have the distraction of having to absorb a new culture or a different set of operating principles. You would also know who's who. If you're unhappy with your current work discipline, this can be a good way for you to find a more suitable area.

A similar role in a new organisation

This is perhaps the easiest proposition to take to the external job marketplace, as employers tend to be fairly conservative when assessing who they want to join their company. If they're looking for a Finance Director and you're already the Finance Director of a similar enterprise, you're much more likely to succeed than a Finance Manager from a completely different sector who's looking for a promotion.

A new role in a new organisation

Hard on the heels of the easiest proposition to take to the external job marketplace is the hardest proposition. It *is* possible to change career direction and companies at the same time, but you'll need to work hard at it and be very convincing and persuasive about why you're trying to make the move and your ability to perform the new role effectively.

32. Glass ceiling?

It's easier to get to the top if you are a man than if you're a woman. Here are some thoughts about how to deal with discrimination.

The statistics are depressing if you're a woman. Look at the number of female MPs; look at the tiny number of women who make it to the boardroom and the number of female CEOs of blue-chip companies. Look at this as a personal challenge, not a male plot. And don't try and change the world single-handedly: your job here is to get to the top, not to make the world a better place.

Managers are prejudiced against women of childbearing age: if they have children they may have to take some time off to look after them; if they do not already have children then they may take maternity leave in order to start a family. Interestingly, the discriminators are not only men, but also women who themselves have opted not to have children in their thirties. So when it

Here's an idea for you...

Mothers who work outside the home say that childcare problems are probably more stressful and difficult to manage than their actual jobs. If a woman knows her kids are being well looked after then she is likely to perform better. Suggesting improvements to your organisation's arrangements – if any – could be a career step, especially if you are proposing it to a woman.

Defining idea...

'Women who seek to be equal with men lack ambition.'
THOMAS LEARY, psychologist

comes to your CV, leave the kids out of the equation. If you are asked if you intend to have children – you shouldn't be, but it still happens – then you might hint at the fact that you are going to channel your energies into a career rather than a family. Economy with the truth is the preferred tactic of many women.

There are two other options if you want a family. Put off becoming a parent until your forties (this can carry some risks, though you can always freeze your eggs) or have children and get your partner to stay at home while you cultivate your career.

Finally, smack down the people who defend the current situation. They tend to say that maternity leave and taking time off for the kids discriminates against shareholders by damaging the profits of the organisation. This can't be true, can it? For a start it seems more damaging to the shareholders to ignore the talents of half the managers in the relevant age group. (Remember there are some male managers whose general incompetence would probably kill a baby left in their charge, so goodness knows what they are doing to their businesses.) And who are these shareholders? In the end most shareholders are people building pension funds or are pensioners themselves. If there are more men building pension funds than women, then this is a result of this discrimination, and there are certainly more women pensioners than men. Pensioners live off the equities built up in their pension funds; therefore giving equal rights to women managers cannot damage the interests of shareholders. QED.

33. Come back in the morning

Know when to put things on the back-burner, and how to let them simmer there.

The fact is everyone works more effectively after a good night's sleep. Fair enough, if it's getting late but you're motoring and 'in the zone', then stay up and feed off that feeling. Fair enough too if you have a deadline and simply must produce *something* for the next day. But never, ever bother bashing away at a problem late at night just for the sake of it, when you know in your heart of hearts you're not really solving anything. That really is a waste of time. And nobody will be impressed with your tired, haggard expression unless the work itself has clearly been worth the effort.

In most cases, admitting defeat and coming back to something in the morning can really help not only to finally complete a piece of

Here's an idea for you...

If you have an imminent deadline, it can actually be really good to take your half-finished work to the meeting, admit your problems and ask for help in fixing them. Sometimes this makes everybody feel creative and valued. (Be careful how often you try and get way with this, by the way.) If your deadline is not so urgent, best leave it for several mornings (or months)!

work in a good way – but also can ensure that you're in some kind of condition to really deliver at the critical moments. If you expend all your energy working fruitlessly through the night, you really aren't going to stand much chance in the morning – either you'll be in bed fast asleep or you'll turn up at the office with your brain about as functional as a boiled pomegranate.

It really is true that you can see things differently in the morning light, especially if you're well rested and alert. Indeed, changes in light generally can throw a very different slant on your work. Test it: try working in different types of light, both artificial and natural. Experiment with a range of different light bulbs, perhaps. At different times of the day move to different rooms that have more or fewer windows, or face in a particular direction. Get up really early and sample the light at dawn, but don't stay up to do the same thing. Similarly, try working at dusk.

Sleep can also bring with it all kinds of strange dreams and thoughts that may come to your aid in the morning. It's amazing, too, how a problem can go away just by letting time pass. For most creative people it's tempting to think that things only happen because of your presence and your input. But actually things happen without you too. Plants still grow, the world still spins and often what seemed so awful yesterday isn't so bad today.

Defining idea...

'Why is it I get my best ideas in the morning while I'm shaving?'
ALBERT EINSTEIN

Crucially, you may also find that if you leave something, somebody else will come along with the necessary input to fix things.

34. Well read

You need talent, artistry, political awareness and opportunism to enjoy the best your career can offer...

You also need knowledge. This knowledge is much wider than your own industry. Here's how to get what you need to know.

Read external sources widely on and around your subject

A director of a large company was asked what made his MD so successful. 'I'm not sure,' said the director, 'but I do know that he's in his office every evening until about 9.30 p.m.' 'What on earth is he doing?' the director was asked. 'Well, reading mainly,' he

Here's an idea for you...

Get a copy of your annual report and the annual report of your main competitor. Do some financial analysis of the two companies and see who is in the better state and why. If you cannot do this, go and see a friendly financial controller and ask them to help you, and give you some advice about how to improve your financial awareness.

responded. 'He keeps up to date with everything there is to read about the business climate, his industry and his customer's industry.'

Then broaden your knowledge base

If you don't usually read a newspaper, get into the habit now. Try *The Economist* or *New Scientist* for a change. Perhaps a tabloid could give you some pointers on popular culture and what people are buying in droves.

Improve your internal economic and financial knowledge

Finance Directors have at their disposal loads and loads of jargon, calculated and correctly worded, all to wrong-foot any up-and-coming manager. When you are promoted to a new job, you have to make sure that you understand the financial implications of what you are required to do, and what criteria you'll be judged by. Or would you rather compete with one hand tied behind your back?

It's a vicious circle. If you ignore the financial side of your job you'll start to lose control of the physical task. If you get behind with the administration it's only going to get worse. You must query figures that appear to be wrong, particularly cross charges coming in from other parts of the business, or you could find yourself carrying a huge load of costs dumped on you by someone who has learnt their way around the system and has seen you coming. Even if there is no one in your organisation with such evil intent, you must not rely on internal costing systems; they are very difficult to get right and are notoriously inaccurate. The main difficulty is to make the systems keep up with changes in the organisation.

The point in the end, of course, concerns decision-making. You can make a decision that seems correct for the organisation but is financially wrong and vice versa. If you combine your functional skills with an understanding and knowledge of the financial consequences of your decisions, then you are on your way to a great career.

35. Handling rejection

A rejection letter needn't be the end of the story. A good follow-up strategy can keep you in the corporate mind's eye.

Picture this scenario. You've had the interview.
It seemed to go well and you came away thinking that you could enjoy working there. You go home and await the outcome of the

Here's an idea for you...

interview only to be told that the organisation has opted to go for another candidate. At this point, you can opt for one of three dispositions:

■ Take it on the chin and focus on the next application.
■ Unleash a volley of bile to the effect that the interviewer and, in fact, the entire company should be dropped down a sizeable hole and forgotten about until the end of time.
■ Turn rejection into an opportunity to build something for the future.

The first two are both understandable, but they treat a rejection as the end of the road. The third suggests that all may not be lost. Success in the job search process is typically not about being head and shoulders above all other candidates – it's about striving to be a few per cent better than the competition every step of the way.

Examples of how to gain that advantage include having a CV that conveys your experience and achievements more effectively, researching a company that bit more thoroughly, being that bit better prepared for the interview, making a better first impression at interview than others, and – critically in this context – following up key stages of the selection process more effectively than others.

Defining idea...

'That which does not kill me makes me stronger.'
NIETZSCHE

If you're not offered a particular job, think seriously about asking for some feedback on your performance. You could also write to the interviewer(s). Perhaps send something along the lines of: 'Thank you for letting me know the outcome of my recent interview. Obviously I'm disappointed not to have been offered the job, as I would have greatly relished taking on this challenging and exciting role. I'd like to take this chance to reaffirm my genuine interest in your organisation and to ask you to bear me in mind for any suitable vacancies that might arise in the future.'

Gratuitous toadying? No – you're simply bringing this particular episode to a close whilst leaving channels of communication open. The organisation will think well of you and you never know what might come of it. For a whole host of reasons the vacancy may reoccur. If this happens, then obviously there are no guarantees, but at least you've left yourself well positioned for the organisation to come back to you.

36. Culture club

You really are looking for compatibility. If the culture's not right, you'll eventually hate the job.

Regardless of how well you fit the job and the job fits you, the thing that makes the organisation successful and you happy is the culture. It's the context within which everyone works. Use the interview to check that you understand the way they work and that you'll enjoy fitting into it. For example, if you're a very creative person don't go for a company that's very process-driven and where strict attention to the rules and the small print is part of their function. So define the elements of an organisation's culture that concern you. Here are some cultural attributes to help you to do this.

Bureaucratic vs. meritocratic and open. On one end of this scale is the organisation that normally promotes through length of time in the job. The mark of a meritocracy is that high-fliers are put into challenging positions at the first opportunity. Openness tends to go with meritocratic.

Internal vs. external focus. Do you want to work in an environment where your plans are pretty much dictated by the level above you, or do you want to drive your plans by thinking about what the external customer wants?

Quality/cost balance. Do you want to work in Rolls Royce, or do you want to work for a company that's increasing its efficiency so much that they can offer good products to a mass market?

Freedom vs. process and control. Are you a risk-taking maverick who likes to spot an opportunity, go for it and ask permission afterwards? If so, you're not going to be comfortable in an environment where any step out of line is met with tutting noises. Many people are more comfortable in an organisation that lets them know precisely where they are and what their sphere of operation and influence will be.

Fun vs. serious. What does it feel like when you walk in the door and talk to people? Some organisations take themselves less seriously than others.

Open vs. closed communication. Do they give a lot of information to a wide audience, or do they inform only those who need to know?

Team vs. individual. Does the organisation operate through its teams, or through its individuals?

Now mark on a scale of 1–10 how you think the organisation you're applying to works against your list of attributes. Also mark on a scale of 1–10 how the culture suits you. Where you can't answer the question through lack of knowledge, make a note to ask a question in that area at the interview. Be wary, though. Sometimes companies proclaim their culture as one thing but act in a completely opposite way.

37. Eight potentially life-changing seconds

On average, it takes eight seconds to decide whether to continue reading a CV. Here's how to capture and keep the reader's attention in those first vital moments.

The fact is, if you can't convince the reader that you're well worth an interview by the time they're midway down page one of your CV, it's unlikely they'll read much further. Think of the first half of page one as your prime selling space. Your aim should be to try to feature all of your major arguments for being interviewed in that space.

There's no point in introducing a new and compelling piece of information halfway down the second page of your CV, as chances are the reader won't reach that point and so it won't be noticed.

So, what's the best information to put on that first half page? Well, virtually all recruiters expect to see your name and contact details at the top of the first page. Not just your name, address and home telephone number, by the way. You should also include your mobile number and an email address, as these are good indicators of your technological literacy.

After your contact details, I'd recommend including a two- or three-line profile statement. Think of it as a sixty- to eighty-word précis of what you have to offer that would make you a prime contender for the position you're going for.

By the time you've included contact details and a profile statement, you should still have around a half to two-thirds of that first half page still available. What follows the profile will vary according to which elements of your background and experience most closely match what the recruiter is looking for. If they're trying to recruit somebody who can do A, B and C, then you'll need to show explicit evidence of your attainments in and experience of doing A, B and C. If this evidence can best be shown in your current/most recent role, then you'll probably want to go straight into your career history. If, on the other hand, you need to draw on your broader career and experience to prove your competence at A, B and C, a section called something like 'Key Achievements' or 'Key Skills and Experience' would suit your purpose better.

Recruiters are only likely to read on beyond this first portion of your CV if they're convinced you explicitly meet the specification they're recruiting against. This is not the time for subtlety. Above all, don't rely on the recruiter to draw inferences from the information you provide. Concentrate on filling that first half page with as much relevant information as you can, paying particular attention to addressing the job and person requirements that the recruiter has stated. Given this, it goes without saying that to feature a piece of information that the recruiter is likely to regard as irrelevant is a definite no-no.

38. Winging a meeting

There's a good reason why we don't prepare for meetings: we don't have time. Seriously. Don't bother.

The Wharton Center for Applied Research recently found that the average senior executive spends 23 hours a week in meetings. If we prepared for meetings properly, there wouldn't be enough time left in the day to hold them. And if we did all the preparation and called all the people we should have done, chances are we would have solved the problem already, rendering the meeting even more useless.

Yet convention demands that when attending a meeting you look like you have put in some work, especially if you called it. If you are in charge, the most important thing about running a meeting is to create a detailed agenda. Keep a standard agenda template: comments from last meeting, unresolved issues, input from departments/working groups/key

Here's an idea for you...

If you want to arrive late and/or leave early, keep one of those small suitcases with wheels on it and bring it to the meeting. Quietly park it in plain view. A late arrival means you just got off a plane or train. An early departure means that you really have to get to the airport or station right away. Your very presence will seem like you're doing everyone a favour.

Defining idea...

contributors, suggestions for next steps, any other business and date of next meeting. Then all you have to do is add the correct date, the title of the meeting and the names of people you want to speak against each item. This name is never you. The other attendees will be so busy looking for their initials that they won't spot that it is the same agenda as last time.

If you are not running the meeting, but expect to be named on the list of people who will contribute content, the important thing is to convince everyone that you have a lot to say while saying as little as possible. Bring a long typed list (any typed list will do as long as it consists of at least ten points) to every meeting. Don't let anyone else see the detail on it. When it's your turn, pick it up and scan carefully. Hearts will sink until you check your watch, glance at the agenda, and say 'In the interests of time, I'll skip most of this, and just cover a few essential points.'

In any meeting designed to decide something, there will usually be The Expert, the one person who knows what he or she is talking about. It would have been much better for everyone if The Expert had been allowed to get on with making the decision alone, but it's important to have a meeting so that you can contribute by agreeing with everything he or she says, and maybe steal some of the credit as a result. Accomplish this by identifying that meeting's Expert, preferably on the way in to the meeting, and engage in friendly banter, which might reveal what point of view The Expert holds. The Expert's aura of capability will extend to you.

39. Life's a balance

It's your choice whether to be a workaholic or not.

You could pursue your career at the expense of all other activities, or you could place a higher priority on family and leisure. You decide. Whatever you choose, here is a way of calculating whether you have the balance as you want it, or whether you have to make some changes.

Firstly, check the situation now. Penny Ferguson, an inspiring trainer, has this simple but effective

Here's an idea for you...

Here's another of Penny Ferguson's techniques. Produce a vision for yourself by writing a description of the best six months of your life that you could have. Really dream and then go back to the activity matrix and plan to achieve that vision. Ask yourself what you need to do to get this plan off the ground. You have made a decision about your work/life balance; so commit now to implementing the changes.

Defining idea...

idea for checking your life/work balance.

There are 168 hours in the week, of which you spend 56 in bed. This leaves 112 for living in. Draw a three by three matrix of nine square boxes and write an activity heading in each of them. This will be your 'activity matrix'. The headings will include some of the following: friends, relationships, family, alone time, spirituality, personal growth, health, hobbies, leisure, creativity, work – operations or maintenance, work – strategic thinking and planning, and any other areas of life that you enjoy or endure. If you need more squares just add them. Don't forget to add areas where at the moment you do nothing but which you wish to get involved in at some future time.

Now list the number of hours in a typical week you spend in each of these areas, convert it to a percentage of 112 and write the percentage into the appropriate box. That's your starting point. You may wish to check what you have written with your partner and a work colleague to make sure you are not indulging in wishful thinking. If the percentages are just what you want, well done.

If they're not, then plan the situation for the future. If you're not entirely happy with the result, look at the areas where you want to make any adjustments. For every area where you raise the percentage you have to make a choice as to which area you are going to decrease. Add in any activities that currently you don't do, but which you would like to, and resolve to get started on them. Now translate the percentages into hours and see if you believe you have a feasible plan. Finally, put it into practice!

40. How to love the job you've got

Sometimes you can't have the one you want. So you have to love the one you've got.

Hate your job? It's probably for three reasons – you hate the work, the environment – including your colleagues – or something else has happened in your life that makes work seem meaningless and you're ready for a lifestyle change. Or it could be that you're in denial. Sometimes we hate our jobs because we can't be bothered to address what's really stressing us out in our lives. Our energy is focused elsewhere. So here are some short and long-term solutions.

Here's an idea for you...

Boost work morale in a stressful workplace by starting group traditions beyond getting drunk on Friday night and moaning. Go out for a Chinese on pay day or book an awayday at a spa or have a whip-round every birthday and celebrate with champagne and cake.

Love your surroundings...

...just as much as you can. If your workplace is grim and dreary, you are not going to feel good. Clear your desk. Sort out clutter. Personalise your work space with objects of beauty and grace. Pin up photos of beautiful vistas you've visited or would like to visit. (It's a bit less personal than family pics.) But whatever you choose to put on your desk, change the visuals every couple of weeks otherwise your brain stops registering them.

Love your lunchbreaks

A break shouldn't be a scramble for bad food and a desultory walk round a shopping mall. Spend time planning. Every lunch hour should involve movement, fresh air, delicious healthy food and at least one work of art. Always, always take your time to relax at lunch.

Love your colleagues

If there are people who specifically annoy you, then find a way to deal with them. Allow yourself no more than five minutes a day unloading your woes about work colleagues to a trusted friend or partner – not anyone you work with. The more you unload your negativity all over the place, the more you are talking yourself into a hole of unhappiness and stress.

Love yourself

Turn up. Work hard. Do better. Lots
of people who are unhappy with
their work kid themselves that they
are working really hard, when in fact
their work is shoddy and second-rate.

If you're not up to speed, improve your knowledge base and skills. Look
at everything you produce or every service you offer and ask yourself
how you can make it special, imbue it with your uniqueness, breathe
creativity and a little bit of love into it. Doing every task diligently and
positively will vastly increase your self-esteem.

Love your dreams

For five minutes in every hour allow yourself to dream. Read through
job pages that aren't related to your present job. You may see a position
or course that fires your imagination in a completely new direction.

41. Who are they?

**Find out about your next potential
employer and target your CV.**

Here are five ways to carry out the research
required to separate the Enrons of this world from the pick of the bunch:

Here's an idea for you...

Remember that the company you go on to join will be the company that will take pride of place at the head of your CV the next time you make a move. How do you think that will play with future employers? Will they be impressed?

Phone a friend

Start putting the word around and you may track down somebody (or somebody who knows somebody) who either works for the company or is a customer or supplier of theirs. These informal sources of information can be an invaluable guide to what's really going on inside the company.

Research them online

The amount of information to be found on the internet is quite staggering. In the pre-internet days, it could be quite difficult to research a company. Nowadays, to turn up at an interview without a detailed understanding of the company is almost unforgivable.

The company website

Most companies of any kind of size will have one. Many of the best sites include an online copy of annual reports, information on company structures, copies of vision or mission statements, press releases and links to related sites. If you don't know the website address, it's always worth trying www.[name of company].co.uk or .com. Failing that, a decent search engine should get you there pretty quickly. If there isn't a company website, that in itself carries a bit of a message.

Get hold of an annual report

You can often do this online via the company's website. There are also a number of ordering services you can use. Alternatively, phone the companies direct and ask them to send you a copy.

Defining idea...

'To be conscious that you are ignorant is a great step to knowledge.'
BENJAMIN DISRAELI

Track newspapers and journals

Scan the newspapers if you can, particularly the broadsheets and business journals like *The Economist*. If something is in the papers, chances are that the topic may well be high in the minds of people who work there.

You should be able to directly incorporate some of the information you uncover into your CV or covering letter. In fact, this should be a specific aim of yours, as there's real added value in letting the company know that you've put time and effort into finding out about them. And, of course, should you be invited to interview, you'll already have done a lot of the legwork to prepare yourself for that part of the selection process.

One final point. Leaving one job for another is a significant life decision. An informed decision is always likely to yield a better outcome than a leap into the dark. Before you think of resigning, are you confident that you know enough about the new role and the new company, such as its culture, the state of the balance sheet, and so on?

42. Finding the perfect boss

You don't want to end up with a boss you can't stand or, worse still, can't stand you.

You're likely to be asked about your relationship with your boss in any interview. The interface with your manager comes in three main areas: agreeing objectives and tasks, solving internal and external problems, and your personal and career development. Here are some ideas.

Let's start with agreeing objectives. Explain that you like a very thorough briefing on what you're supposed to achieve. 'I want to work for someone who is interested enough in the detail of what I do to ensure that I have a comprehensive knowledge of my project. I also like to know how my project fits into the whole divisional and company strategy. I much prefer tightly-written objectives that make it clear whether or not I'm on the way to achieving the right results.'

Now think about what you want out of them in terms of problem solving. 'I like to be able to go to my boss with a problem whenever I judge the time is right. I also like it if they expect me to come with some analysis of the problem – I tend to list the strengths, weaknesses, opportunities and threats that arise from the situation. I also like to work for someone who encourages me to come up with my own recommendations for what we

Here's an idea for you...

Try to research the actual person you'll be working for. Talk to one of their colleagues or preferably someone whose opinion you value who works for them. Plainly, this is more likely to happen in an internal promotion.

should do. That preparation work should make the manager's task easier. If you don't present the problem in that way, you're just alerting them that something's going wrong and letting them work out what to do. I expect them to give me a fair amount of protection from company politics, and I certainly hope they'll keep making sure that what I'm doing is good for the whole organisation.'

Venture a little bit now towards the relationship between the two of you. 'It's very important to me that our relationship is very open and that we can say what we like to each other without causing hurt or animosity. We need to stay positive with each other: I find that then it just works, and the relationship develops well.'

You might be asked how you like to get feedback. The quick answer is 'All the time, and given in a way that allows me to exploit my strengths and work on my weaknesses.' The longer answer looks at your career development.

A summary of your ideal boss would go like this: 'My ideal manager works in an open manner and with integrity. They make sure I understand what I have to do and fully support my endeavours.'

When asked negative questions like 'Does your current boss do anything you dislike?' a possible approach might be: 'Well, I'm not sure that "dislike" is the right word and it seems to be working better now, but...'

43. Manage the brand called You

What makes you so special?

'It's this simple: you are a brand. You are in charge of your brand. There is no single path to success. And there is no one right way to create the brand called You. Except this: Start today. Or else.' That's a quote from Tom Peters, probably the world's best known management guru, in an article he wrote for *Fast Company*. Our personal brand value can rise or fall depending on how well we nurture our brand and how well we perform in the marketplace.

You may cringe at the thought of being 'a brand called You', but behind this clodhopping language rests a new truth about what lies ahead for everyone looking to change jobs. Getting a new job isn't the challenge. Finding the right job *is*, however. Whether you're contemplating an internal or external move, you need to make sure that it keeps your career moving in an upward trajectory. Choose the right employer and that can increase your brand value. Choose the wrong employer and you can do lasting damage to your earning potential. So, what can we do to protect our careers?

Here's an idea for you...

Ask yourself the following deceptively simple question to help you define your brand: What do I want to be famous for? Then ask yourself what needs to happen next in order for you to get closer to your chosen brand identity.

The general assumption seems to be that performing well in a given job is all that matters; look after your job and somehow your career will take care of itself. Not true. Building a long and successful career requires a 'planned maintenance' mentality. Don't assume that combining patience with a dollop of opportunism will do the trick – bugger all comes to they who wait.

Don't entrust your career to anybody. Don't rely on the company's Management Development Manager or VP-Succession Planning to look after your interests – they have other fish to fry. And don't rely on your current boss to look after your best interests. All too many managers are very happy to keep their good people for as long as they possibly can.

Finally, don't imagine that the skills, knowledge and experience that got you where you are today will be sufficient to propel you where you want to be in the future. Seek out opportunities to acquire new skills, become a voracious learner and develop career purpose. People with a vision of their future and goals linked to that vision are far more likely to succeed than those without.

44. Lead with style

The ultimate test of leadership is the top job.

Good senior managers can smell a well-motivated, happy team from a mile off. The team members exude confidence. They work hard and make sacrifices. They display pride in their work and in their membership of what they honestly believe is the best bit of the organisation. Not only that, but everyone, including Human Resources, will know that people are queuing up to get into that team. So, how do you create this aura?

Some say leaders are born and cannot be created, and it's true that your basic ability to get on with people is, to some extent, your starting point for being a leader. But there are a number of leadership techniques that develop your natural ability to make things happen. Think about motivation – leadership is the skill of persuading people to co-operate *willingly* to achieve results. The 'willingly' is key: you cannot force motivation on people; they have to want to do a good job. Motivation occurs when people feel that they're able to make their very best contribution.

Here's an idea for you...

At your next team meeting take the role of chairman absolutely seriously on at least one important topic. Do not make any proposals for possible actions yourself or appear to support any particular view. Let the team decide what to do, summarise their plan, and thank them for their hard work and good thinking.

Some people talk about 'push and pull' management styles. Push is the 'Do what you are told' or autocratic method; pull is the consulting, democratic way of leading people. You need a combination of the two for different people and in different situations. So your team leadership style can range from giving simple directives to group discussion and consensus. If you tend too much towards giving directions you will, among other things, stifle the creativity of the team. That in turn reduces the number of times you will be able to take a good new idea to your boss. There is almost nothing that boosts a career more than being the first to make an innovative idea work and having it taken up by the rest of the company. Everybody will want to talk to you about it.

Finally, always remember that people work for money but will do a bit extra for recognition, praise and reward. Show appreciation often. Don't wait for the end of a task to say thank you. It is often a good idea to thank someone in the middle of a project for getting on with it without having to involve you.

So, show a genuine interest in other people, communicate well and pick the right style at the right time and you will lead with style.

45. Be an achiever

A substantial record of personal achievements is more important than an impressive job description.

An achievement-based CV will give a potential employer a clear idea of the impact that you might have if recruited. If you're planning to enter the job market in the near future you therefore need to be able to build into your CV an impressive set of achievements. We often don't give ourselves credit for the skills and abilities we have built up over the years and instead take them for granted. So here's a quick exercise to help you see how good you are at recognising your achievements.

■ Write down thirty or so achievements that you're really proud of. If listing thirty achievements sounds excessive, please persevere. By the time you're up to achievement 23, you'll start surprising yourself with all you've done that had slipped from immediate recollection.

Here's an idea for you...

Rate thirty or so achievements in terms of the likely impact they'll have on a recruiter. Ask yourself which are the strongest examples and aim to use those rather than their weaker counterparts.

- Alongside each achievement, make a note of the underlying skills or abilities you drew on in order to succeed.
- Armed with the output from this exercise, you should get a pretty good idea of the skills and abilities you can take into the job marketplace.

Bear in mind that achievements are contextual – in other words, our work environment and the corporate culture that we're part of shape what's expected of us and what it's possible for us to achieve. For example, you may have the capacity to be innovative yet work in an environment that's unsupportive of innovation, such as a risk-averse life assurance company. You may therefore struggle to come up with a work-based example of being innovative. Where this is the case and where you're putting yourself forward for a role that requires innovative thinking, you may need to provide an achievement that drew on innovation from either a previous role or from a non-work situation. It's perfectly legitimate to use such examples in your CV.

The downside with achievements is that – like much of your CV – they have a shelf life. A genuine achievement that goes back ten years or more won't carry as much of an impact as a more recent

example will. You'll need a
demonstrable record of
achievements in order to achieve
your career ambitions. Without it,
your marketability will plummet.

46. Office politics

**Someone who says they're not interested
in office politics is someone who's not
going up the organisation as far as their
talent deserves.**

Good office politicians keep the competition, their management
and colleagues on the back foot by never accepting the existing
organisation as it is. Two great ways to win here – abolish your job
and/or create a completely new one.

One of the things you can do is to make your job redundant: This may
seem a risky process, but it's a great mistake in career planning to
assume that the current management structure is the one in which
you have to succeed.

Here's the reasoning. Many jobs exist because they have always done so, rather than because they represent the best way of getting things done successfully. If you go into a new job and do it the best way for your organisation to succeed, you'll probably find yourself going way outside the original job description. So, your way of operating gets better

results. Now delegate as much of the job as you can in your new way of working and guess what: when you explain what has happened to your boss, they'll realise that they need to change the structure of their operation. If you've done this ploy well, they'll also realise that your tasks are now handled much more efficiently and they don't need you in your old role. Time to move onwards and upwards.

The corollary of abolishing your job, namely inventing a new one, also holds true. People who succeed are the ones who help the organisation keep up to date and help to prevent it ossifying.

It is easier to create a new job if the change helps the organisation achieve better performance, but it's possible to do it for your own purposes alone. The creation of a new job is in two parts. First

Defining idea...

'If the devil doesn't exist, but man has created him, he has created him in his own image and likeness.'
FYODOR DOSTOEVSKY

describe the new way of doing business that will ensure that the job of your dreams is going to exist. Then sell the idea. What you're doing here is showing what your new plan will do in business terms rather than in structural or people terms. Don't reveal your whole hand at this stage because it's too early. Don't give anyone the opportunity to say that what you're doing is for your own greater glory rather than the advancement of the organisation. Having sold the change, produce your implementation plan and, of course, include the new positions required. Then it's time to go for it.

47. Actions speak louder than decisions

If you have taken a decision and informed your boss of what you and your team are going to do, for your career's sake make absolutely sure it happens.

If you haven't started the action plan, you may as well not have made a decision. Consider this.

An elderly painter and decorator who did not want to retire altogether, did want to have more time for himself. Unfortunately for him he is both a great bloke and brilliant at his job, which means that his previous clients, friends and relatives all turn to him when they want work done and he finds it difficult to say no.

Here's an idea for you...

Pick a team member who has difficulty with the 'do it now' concept, someone who tends to agree to a decision and then finds loads of reasons why it can't be implemented. Sit this person down and tell them the story of the painter. Now get them to make a decision and put the actions into their diary.

Remember, a decision is not a decision until there is commitment to action and the first steps are taken. The painter decided to take up golf, and then tried to implement his decision. He resolved to take every Friday off to pursue this new hobby. Four weeks later he had not been able to do so once. Then he committed to a lesson with the professional on the next Friday morning and to another one that afternoon. He paid for the lessons in advance, which broke the deadlock. He started to play, is now something of an addict and plays every Friday. But it wasn't a decision until he'd gone into action.

Right, where is this stuff important? Well, never disappoint the powers that be. Most teams work with some operational targets that they need urgently to achieve. If your team is well organised you'll

115

Defining idea...

*'My choice in everything is to say
nothing and go do it.'*
**LOU GERSTENER, American consultant
and executive, CEO of IBM among
others**

also have a strategic plan that
includes a series of projects aimed
at improving the environment in
which you operate. If you
implement these projects, life will
become easier and performance
will improve. Being career-minded
you will, of course, have told your boss all about the changes the
team is going to make, perhaps with a loud drum roll. But in the
real world pressure is always on maintaining performance rather
than on developing new methods. On average, a boss will ask three
times how you are getting on with the new idea. The third time
your boss hears your excuse that unfortunately there just has not
been time to get it going, they will forget it and write you down as
all mouth and no trousers.

48. Downshifting

**We all fantasise about chucking in the day
job from time to time.**

Over the past ten years or so the downshifting
movement has gained a new lease of life against a backdrop of marked
changes in the world of employment and employability. To more and

more people feeling stressed out by a high-pressure working life, it's become a bit of a fantasy to consider swapping corporately induced misery for a simpler, more satisfying way of life.

Wander around a typical Cornish village these days and you're likely to chance upon former bank employees now running bed and breakfasts, not to mention ex-stockbrokers who have taken up painting.

Here's an idea for you...

If you've moved to a cheaper area as part of your downsizing exercise, it helps if you have a strategy for bonding with the local people. Not paying attention to this side of the equation can cause a measure of resentment with the local population, particularly as the properties that you and other downshifters have bought outright could well be the same houses that the more aspirational villagers are looking to 'upshift' into.

Downshifting implicitly requires the cashing in of resources which have already been acquired, and so it's less suited to those of us in the early stages of our careers and on the lower rungs of the property ladder.

Of course, the decision whether to downshift is not merely a financial one. Here are some key questions that any potential downshifter needs to face:

- Are you really prepared to sacrifice part of your income for a better quality of life?
- Have you tried mapping out a budget for your downsized life to decide if it's feasible? Are you really prepared to go without those

restaurant meals, those nights at the opera, galleries, etc.?
- Where is your downsized income going to come from? Do you need to negotiate reduced hours with your current employers, or are you looking for a completely new income stream? Are you planning to release some capital by selling your old place?

At the heart of a successful downshifting move is a reality-centred understanding of the life and financial changes it will involve. If you are truly prepared to take on all that downshifting entails, you could be heading towards a more satisfying, less financially dependent future. However, it's not for the faint-hearted. Dewy-eyed fantasists need not apply.

49. The seven deadly CV sins

Sometimes best practice is about the things we do; sometimes it's more about the things we don't do...

The biggest CV sin is probably to bore the pants off the reader, but there are plenty of other pitfalls awaiting the inattentive amongst us.

Pride can lead us to overstate our abilities. So, don't go describing your IT skills as 'excellent' when you know little more than how to turn on your PC. Equally, don't enclose a photo because you're damn good-looking, unless you're a model, actor or actress, of course.

Here's an idea for you...

Avoid unnecessary repetition in your CV. Do not repeat things. Say them only once. Do not say them twice. Or three times. Once is enough. (Now can you see how irritating repetition is?)

Avarice can lead us to apply for jobs that are well beyond our capabilities. In truth, we're often more attracted to the salary than to the job itself. The opposite of avarice is generosity. Acknowledging the contributions of others from time to time will demonstrate that you can be a team player.

Envy might come out in the form of sniping at the effort of others, which is a dangerous tactic. Alternatively, we might feel tempted to claim experience and qualifications we don't possess in order to appear on an equal footing with others.

Wrath If we've left or are leaving our current organisation on less than harmonious terms there's a very human tendency to want to express those feelings. Just remember that your CV isn't the right place for this.

Lust causes us to suspend rational judgement in the pursuit of gratification. Remember that you're not obliged to accept the first job offer that comes your way. The offer may be flattering, but feel free to turn it down if it's a poor fit for the criteria you've set for your ideal job.

Gluttony... well, an overindulgent CV gives too much detail and goes on for too many pages. The perfect, moderate CV gives the reader the right amount of information.

Sloth With CV writing, there are two areas where lack of effort will undermine success. The first is where we simply take an old CV and bring it up to date rather than going for a radical overhaul and rewrite. The second is where we don't put enough effort into adapting a CV for each application.

50. Know what to say to whom

A meteoric careerist can't have too much exposure to top people.

You happen to be in the lift with your Chairman, or a senior executive of a major customer. Make sure you know what you would say to them.

Don't blow this short window of time with small talk. There is a clue here for the careerist. But it's not just about the Chairman. You can expand on this by dropping in on anyone. Hewlett Packard used to have a useful slogan: 'managing by wandering around'. It was a neat way of reminding managers that part of their job was to be around and meet people by chance as well as in formal meetings.

Here's an idea for you...

If, for example, you know the boss's diary you'll know when he or she is going to be talking to someone you'd like to meet. First, prepare. If you got the opportunity, what would you say? Then engineer the opportunity to say it. The best way is simply to breeze in. 'Oh, I'm sorry I didn't realise...' 'That's all right,' says your boss, 'Come in and meet So-and-so.' Take it from there.

Try to be in the office at the same time as your boss. After all, in your absence an interesting and potentially rewarding opportunity might be given to someone else. You need to know your boss's diary so that you can plan your absences for times when you won't be missed.

Obviously you want high-level exposure to things that go well. You also want cover against being held responsible for something going wrong. People with moderate ambitions keep a detailed record of their activities with a note of the people who supported them on the way. The more ambitious person with an eye on the big picture does it in such a way that the record can prove that others were completely responsible if it goes wrong. Don't forget to have a shredder handy if all goes well, though. It wouldn't do for you to enable someone else to take the glory.

If you're involved with high-level operations it is generally not a good idea to be closely associated with failure. Stay clear of the firing line unless there are massive points for effort as opposed to achievement.

There is another way of looking at this if the cock-up is really huge. A person in charge of a substantial development project spent £50 million of his company's money on it and was, towards the end, powerless to prevent it having no impact on the business at all. The entire sum was completely wasted. Asked into his boss's office he pre-empted the inevitable by saying that he knew he was there to be fired. 'No way,' said his boss, a very astute woman, 'Now that we have spent £50 million on your learning what doesn't work, we are not about to throw that investment away.' It's a variant of the 'owe your bank £1,000 and it's your problem, owe it a million and it's theirs' situation.

51. Practical interview skills

Two items that often come up in second interviews or assessment centres are in-tray exercises and presentations.

Let's begin with the first possibility. They can simulate your in-tray very dramatically nowadays, with twenty emails in your inbox, your computer buzzing to signal an urgent message and a tray overflowing with paperwork. So be seen to be systematic.

Don't act on the items as they come. Make sure you've read everything before you make any decisions. There could be a snake at the bottom of the pile. It's also likely that one item will have an impact on another. The most popular way of handling an in-tray exercise is, like all great techniques, very simple. Put the paperwork and emails into three categories – A, B, C – by assessing their urgency and impact. 'Urgent' is something's that's got to be done or it'll be too late. 'Impact' measures how much an item affects the profit-and-loss account or other people.

■ A is stuff that you think is urgent, that in real life you would do today – things you're going to deal with during the exercise. Matters to do with customers are most likely to occupy this category.

■ B is stuff that's important but not as urgent as A. You'll get round to these today only if you finish

Here's an idea for you...

Announce at the start of a role-play presentation exactly what you want the group to decide at the end. There's a risk that someone in the audience will tell you it won't be possible to achieve your aim; but it's better to know this at the start than at the end. If you know what the audience's objections are, you may be able to use your presentation to overcome them.

Defining idea...

'Unless one is a genius, it is best to aim at being intelligible.'
SIR ANTHONY HOPE HOSKINS, British novelist

with A. Tomorrow these matters could well go into A.

■ C is material that may still be important. You need to know where it is, so that if something happens that changes its urgency or impact you can promote the item to A or B.

If they interrupt you with phone calls during the exercise, establish quickly who is calling and what their position is. You'll want to speak immediately to your boss, for example, since they may well change at least one of your priorities. When these interruptions occur, make sure that an observer can see you're applying the same systematic rules to each one, and putting those that don't need action now into C, even when someone on the phone says the matter's urgent.

The best tips for making effective presentations are the usual suspects: set tight objectives and talk exclusively in terms the audience will understand. During your preparation, try to put yourself in the audience's shoes. This should help you to use only the language that they use and understand. Don't forget when you're planning your magnificent opening that you've also got to finish with a bang ('er, well, that's about it' is not great). Allow time for questions and think through what the questions are likely to be, so you can respond professionally.

52. Jumping ship

Here's how to get another job with a fat-cat salary when in your current job you've done nothing, nada, nix, and until now you've got away with it.

It's much easier to move on in the same organisation than a new one. But the boss you've got right now thinks you're a skiver. And any potential new manager will ask your current boss for his or her opinion of you. This is much less of a problem than it seems.

Firing someone is very hard work and no manager wants to go through the whole bureaucratic rigmarole if they don't have to, and that includes your boss. Think about it from your boss's point of view. The personnel department will find and brandish your last appraisal where the person who's trying to fire you said such nice things about you. They'll make your boss fill in forms, make statements and struggle through a long series of verbal warnings, written warnings, having witnesses at the meetings, offering you the chance to have a witness at the meetings and so forth. No one wants to do this.

OK, you've searched the house magazine and found a new job that's suitable. It's a bit more money (nobody believes that anyone

Here's an idea for you...

An appraisal is an important document to be used in evidence as you pursue your route to the top without actually doing anything. Think about the wording with the HR department in mind. All you need is to make sure it says that you've done what you were expected to do and that you're a loyal servant of the organisation. Those are the two things employment tribunals are looking for.

voluntarily moves sideways) but it's not so much that it would make your old boss jealous or even hopping mad. You've gone to the interviews and knocked their socks off. There's only one small cloud on the horizon – the new people are bound to talk to your boss. Get your retaliation in first.

Talk to your boss. You have two objectives. First, help him or her to understand that you're not likely to give up easily if they try to sink you. Make it quite clear that you're not going to go quietly. This one is going to end in court and they're going to have to explain to a lot of people why they didn't realise that you've done absolutely bugger all for two whole years. Now find some positives. Why is the new job more suitable for your talents? Remember: they're looking for reasons to advance your case; they've already decided to avoid the pain of sacking you. Think about this reference business before you choose your new manager. Anyone your boss hates is a good candidate; your boss will want to hack them off. Anyone your boss doesn't know can also be the right person.

brilliant ideas

Find your dream job: 52 brilliant little ideas for total career happiness is published by Infinite Ideas, creators of the acclaimed 52 Brilliant Ideas series. If you found this book helpful, you may want to take advantage of this special offer exclusive to all readers of *Find your dream job*. Choose any two books from the selection below and you'll get one of them free of charge*. See overleaf for prices and details on how to place your order.

- **Downshift to the good life:** Scale it down and live it up
- **Inspired creative writing:** 52 brilliant ideas from the master wordsmiths
- **Whole health:** Inspirational ideas for mind and body well-being
- **Unleash your creativity:** Secrets of creative genius
- **Upgrade your brain:** 52 brilliant ideas for everyday genius
- **Look gorgeous always:** 52 brilliant ideas to find it, fake it and flaunt it
- **Healthy cooking for children:** 52 brilliant ideas to dump the junk
- **Smarter business start-ups:** Start your dream business

For more detailed information on these books and others published by Infinite Ideas please visit www.infideas.com

*Postage at £2.75 per delivery address is additional.

Choose any two titles from below and receive one of them free.

Qty	Title	RRP
	Downshift to the good life	£12.99
	Inspired creative writing	£12.99
	Whole health	£12.99
	Unleash your creativity	£12.99
	Upgrade your brain	£12.99
	Look gorgeous always	£12.99
	Healthy cooking for children	£12.99
	Smarter business start-ups	£12.99

Subtract £12.99 if ordering two titles

Add £2.75 postage per delivery address

Final TOTAL

Name: ....

Delivery address: ....

....

....

E-mail:................................Tel (in case of problems): ....

By post Fill in all relevant details, cut out or copy this page and send along with a cheque made payable to Infinite Ideas. Send to: *Find your dream job BOGOF*, Infinite Ideas, 36 St Giles, Oxford OX1 3LD. **Credit card orders over the telephone** Call +44 (0) 1865 514 888. Lines are open 9am to 5pm Monday to Friday. Just mention the promotion code 'FYDJAD06.'

Please note that no payment will be processed until your order has been dispatched. Goods are dispatched through Royal Mail within 14 working days, when in stock. We never forward personal details on to third parties or bombard you with junk mail. This offer is valid for UK and RoI residents only. Any questions or comments please contact us on 01865 514 888 or email info@infideas.com.